Contents

Standard Grade Administration

This course is designed to enable you to acquire knowledge, skills and understanding of administration and to develop your ability to use information and communications technology to process information.

 You will be assessed on your Knowledge and Understanding (KU), which is your ability to recall, describe and explain facts and ideas related to all aspects of administration.

 You will also be expected to Problem-Solve (PS). PS questions ask you to suggest solutions to given problems by using your knowledge of administration procedures.

Assessment

These two areas are assessed by an external examination at either General or Credit level, and some of you may sit both levels.

General Paper	Credit Paper
The **General Paper** lasts for 1 hour and 15 minutes.	The **Credit Paper** lasts for 1 hour and 30 minutes.
KU questions make up 30 marks. PS questions make up 30 marks.	KU questions make up 32 marks. PS questions make up 33 marks.
A workbook is provided at General level to help you to complete your answers.	

A third part of the course, which is not covered in this book, is the Practical Abilities project. The Practical Abilities project tests your ICT skills, and you will do a project in class time at school as your assessment for this part of the course.

The overall award for the course is worked out on the average grade for each part.

KU questions are worth 30% of your final grade.
PS questions are worth 30% of your final grade.
The PA project counts for 40% of your final grade.

How this book will help you

If you are studying Standard Grade Administration and want to get a good grade at either General or Credit level, then this book is for you. Each of the seven topics in the Standard Grade course has been clearly identified and summarised. There is also a selection of the most common types of exam questions appearing at each level.

There are suggested answers to every question, with advice on how best to tackle each question. In addition, there are key pointers ('Look out for!' sections) which give advice on how to avoid common mistakes, follow best practice and gain the most marks possible.

Study tips

If you are sitting this course at both levels, you need to be clear about the differences in the type of answers to give – make sure you read the advice given for each question. As both papers are timed, be aware of how long you are taking to answer the questions, and try not to fall into the trap of writing too much at the start and not being able to complete the paper.

Finally, throughout the book you are reminded to read the key words in the question. This is extremely important. Look at the marks allocated to questions – this is the best hint as to how much you have to write. Try to answer in sentences and avoid giving one-word answers, as one-word answers tend not to get many (if any) marks.

Plan your revision time carefully, and do a little regularly – leaving it all until the night before the exam is really not a good idea.

Organisation of departments

What you need to know at General level …

You need to know about the

- purpose of organisation charts
- interpretation of organisation charts
- levels of responsibility in the chart
- chains of command.

YOU ARE HERE

Many business organisations will use an organisation chart to inform staff, customers and visitors of the structure of the organisation.

These charts are usually displayed in the reception area and will show the main departments of the organisation, the job titles and staff working in the departments, the relationships and responsibilities, the chain of command and span of control.

The charts will also show whether the organisation has a tall or a flat structure.

General question 1 –

a) State two advantages of a tall organisational structure.

1 *A tall structure will have more levels of management.*

2 *It will also have a narrow span of control.*

b) An organisation wishes to make its chart more meaningful to staff and visitors. Suggest two ways it could do this.

1 *Pictures of the staff*

2 *Colour coding of departments*

*In this type of question, you will be expected to show that you know the advantages and disadvantages of each type of structure, and you should know at least **two** of each. The answer book will guide you to make sure that you give two clear advantages.*

You should know that organisation charts are diagrams which become more informative with the use of pictures and labels. Again, you are guided by the answer book as to how much to write.

Look out for

It is important to learn the specific terminology associated with organisation charts.

General question 2 –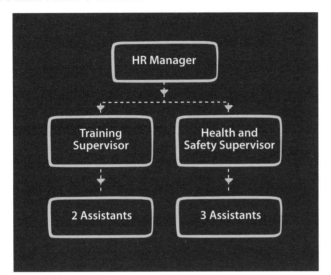

HUMAN RESOURCES DEPARTMENT

```
HR Manager
    │
    ├──────────────────────┐
    ▼                      ▼
Training              Health and
Supervisor        Safety Supervisor
    │                      │
    ▼                      ▼
2 Assistants          3 Assistants
```

a) Explain what is meant by the chain of command.

   The chain of command shown in this chart is the line of
   authority from the HR Manager down to the Supervisor,
   down to the Assistants.

b) Identify who is sharing a lateral relationship in this chart.
   The Training Supervisor and Health and Safety Supervisor.

c) Describe the biggest disadvantage of using organisation charts.

   The main disadvantage of organisation charts is the fact that
   they go out of date very quickly as people leave or join the
   organisation.

Chain of command shows the lines of authority and responsibility, so you would need to identify that information and instructions are passed down from the HR Manager to Supervisors and then to Assistants. If you are unsure about levels of responsibility, always follow the lines down the chart. This type of relationship is known as a *line relationship*. The more subordinates who report to a manager, the larger that manager's *span of control*. Where members of staff are on the same level in the chart, this is a *lateral relationship*.

However, sometimes one member of staff may have a greater span of control than another. This can be seen in the case of the Health and Safety Supervisor, as they have more staff reporting to them than the Training Supervisor.

! Look out for

Check the wording of the question, as sometimes you will be asked to give the benefits of organisation charts to the visitor, to the organisation itself, or to employees. Make sure your answer is for the correct one.

General question 3 – 📖

Organisation charts are important to organisations because they show the 'span of control'.

a) Explain what is meant by **span of control.**

Span of control is the term used to describe the number of
people that a manager has reporting to him/her.

b) Describe two other uses of an organisation chart for **employees**.

1 *Employees can see the lines of reporting and channels*
of communication.

2 *Employees can see at a glance the different activities*
within the organisation.

*Although the word **employees** is highlighted in the question above, this may not happen in the actual exam. It is important that your answer in this case does reflect how charts are important to **employees** and not to visitors or others involved with the organisation.*

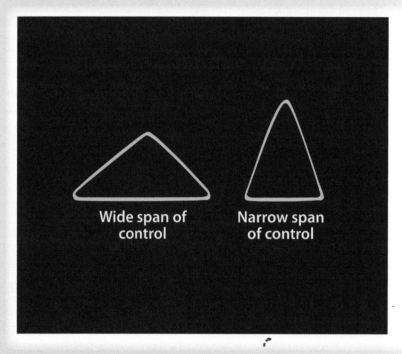

Wide span of control

Narrow span of control

*A **wide** span of control indicates a large number of people, whilst a **narrow** span of control indicates just a few. The diagram shows what this means.*

❗ Look out for

Use words like power/authority/responsibility/
accountability where possible when answering
questions on organisation charts.

What you need to know at **Credit** level ...

In addition to what you need to know at General level, you need to know about

▶ line and lateral relationships

▶ the effects of organisational restructuring on an organisation chart

▶ completing an organisation chart.

Credit question 1 –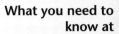

a) Describe two benefits to be gained by an organisation from restructuring, and two problems which could occur once it has been restructured.

b) Outsourcing is often one of the reasons for restructuring. Explain the meaning of this term and identify two other reasons for restructuring.

THEY LAID OFF HALF THE STAFF & INSTALLED MIRRORS HOPING NO ONE WOULD NOTICE

c) After restructuring, organisation charts are often included in staff newsletters and uploaded to the intranet for staff use. Explain why this is the case.

*You should know what **restructuring** means so that you can answer this question. More analysis of questions is expected at Credit level, so you would need to clearly identify the benefits and make sure that you show the problems from a management point of view.*

a) *Benefits of restructuring are reduced staffing costs, greater efficiency in using resources and better lines of communication. Problems associated with restructuring tend to be staff resistance because they have a fear of losing their jobs, and more mistakes made as staff are often new in post.*

b) *Outsourcing means buying in specialist services, possibly because it is cheaper than doing the job yourself. Other reasons for restructuring include reducing layers of management to downsize the organisation or sometimes expanding the organisation and diversifying into different products or services.*

c) *Organisation charts are used to help identify the roles and responsibilities of staff, and by putting them into newsletters this can help to highlight any changes that have taken place. They can show, at a glance, new chains of command and spans of control, allowing employees to see who to contact now.*

Look out for

Remember to use the correct terminology in your answer and **always try to explain your answers**.

Credit question 2 –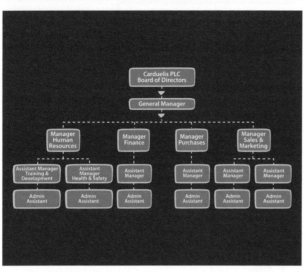

*The key words to part b) of this question are the **promoted staff**. These are the managers in this example.*

At a recent Board Meeting, the Directors decided to centralise the administrative support function and to relocate the six Admin Assistants. The Directors appoint Hollie Shaw as the Administration Manager and Grant Mason as her Assistant Manager. Grant will be responsible for the Admin Assistants in the new department.

a) Draw **only that part of the organisation chart** that will illustrate the **administrative support** function.
b) What effects will this restructuring have on the promoted members of staff?

*As you are asked to draw only **part** of the chart, make sure that this is what you do. You will gain no more marks and will lose time if you draw the whole chart again. Look carefully at the existing layout and make sure you copy the chain of command. Use the names given to you in the question.*

a)
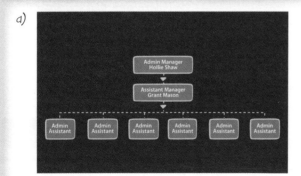

b) *The General Manager's span of control increases from four functional managers to five, and he has a new line relationship.*
- *A new lateral relationship is created with the original functional managers and Hollie Shaw.*
- *The original four Assistant Managers no longer have any responsibility for the Admin Assistants.*
- *Grant Mason, the new Assistant Manager in admin, has the responsibility for six Admin Assistants and a very wide span of control.*

Look out for

In the exam, you will not be asked to construct a complete organisation chart; but at Credit level you may be asked to complete a section, as in the 2007 paper.

Key functions of departments within an organisation

What you need to know at General **level ...**

You need to be able to give

▶ a brief outline of the departments, including the key personnel and key tasks.

Businesses exist to make a profit, and to do this they have to carry out a range of activities. The activities are usually grouped and given to different departments (sometimes called functional areas). The key functions of the business and are usually arranged into:

▶ Sales and Marketing
▶ Purchases
▶ Human Resources (Personnel)
▶ Finance
▶ Administration
▶ Computer Services/ICT.

The advantages to be gained from this functional grouping tend to be:

▶ more efficient use of resources
▶ improved lateral communication between managers
▶ opportunities for team working
▶ clear line relationships.

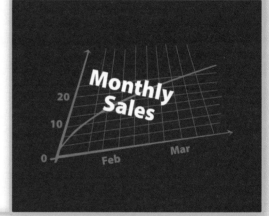

General question 1 –

a) Patterson Enterprises have just advertised the following vacancy
  • Finance Assistant

Describe two tasks which would be carried out in this post.

Task 1 *Updating spreadsheets*

Task 2 *Preparing cheques to be sent to suppliers*

b) Suggest two tasks carried out by the Purchases Manager.

Task 1 *Purchasing materials*

Task 2 *Controlling stock*

c) Describe a spreadsheet task that could be carried out in the Purchases Department.

c) *Recording the details or orders that have been made, adding up totals and calculating VAT.*

Look out for

Human Resources and Personnel perform the same function in organisations.

*When answering this question, it is really important to make sure that you focus on the **Finance** Department in part a). Your answer must specifically mention tasks that an assistant would do in this department – you will get no marks if your answer just covers general admin duties.*

In part b), you should make it clear that you know the role of the Purchases Manager so that you can describe what he/she does.

In part c), you should be able to say what spreadsheets can be used for.

General question 2 –

a) In which department will the following job titles be found? Describe one task which would be performed in each of these roles.

Customer Services Assistant

Department _Sales and Marketing Department_

Task _May have to deal with complaints._

Training Officer

Department _HR Department_

Task _Responsible for organising and delivering courses to staff._

Office Junior

Department _Admin section_

Task _Filing and answering the telephone._

Invoice Clerk

Department _Purchases Department_

Task _Responsible for entering details from invoices into a spreadsheet._

The key to this answer is to ensure that you make specific mention of the correct department and task. Don't just repeat the job title in your answer.

What you need to know at **Credit** **level ...**

In addition to what you need to know at General level, you must

▶ give more detailed answers with regard to the specific tasks and roles within each functional department.

Credit question 1 – 📦

a) One of the main activities of a Human Resources Department is the recruitment of staff. **Explain** and **justify** the use of a Job Description and Person Specification in the recruitment of staff.

a) A job description contains basic information about the job, including the job title, the hours of work, rate of pay, responsibilities, holidays and salary.

The person specification is designed to help identify the type of person required for the job and list the essential and desirable skills and qualities.

A job description can be sent to applicants to give them more details about the job, and to check their suitability for the post.

Both documents help the HR Department to prepare suitable questions for the interview and help to highlight differences between candidates. This will help the HR Department to choose the right person for the job.

*This is an example of the type of question that is often not answered well. The words that are in bold are there to draw your attention to their importance in your answer. **Justify** is a very important word: when you see it, you must state why a course of action has been chosen. So, in this question, as well as explaining the **purpose and content** of each of the two documents, you must also state **why** they are of use to the HR Department.*

Credit question 2 – 📦

a) Explain the role of two functional departments in an organisation.

a) The Sales and Marketing Department is responsible for selling the good or service produced by the organisation. The Marketing part of the department will be responsible for pricing and branding the product, and the Sales part for collecting and processing orders, dealing with enquiries and liaising with the customer.

The Computer Services Department performs an extremely important support function in that it deals with setting up and maintaining the organisation's hardware/software and network.

In this question, you can choose which two functional departments you want to use. You can select from: Sales and Marketing, Finance, Human Resources, Purchases, Computer Services/ICT or Administration.

You have not been asked to quantify how many tasks or activities there are in these departments, so this question would not usually be worth many marks. It would probably form part of another question.

❗ Look out for

You should know the content of more unusual job roles, e.g. IT Support Technician.

Credit question 3 –

a) Describe two activities that would be carried out by the Purchases Department.
b) Identify and explain two documents that would be used in this department.

a) Two activities carried out by the Purchases Department are: getting quotations from suppliers in preparation for ordering goods and services; keeping accurate stock records.

b) Two documents used by the Purchases Department would be an Order Form which would have the names and addresses of the organisation and the supplier, the quantity being ordered, the catalogue code, the price, the VAT and the total cost.

Look out for

Try to make sure that you match up the correct type of task to the correct functional department. You must be **specific** to gain marks in this type of question.

Credit question 4 –

A recent course on Fire Prevention and Evacuation Procedures received poor evaluations from the staff who attended.

Some of the comments included:

• Too much theory and not enough practical information.
• The trainers were not able to answer my question.
• The course was too long and not really relevant to my needs.

a) Which department should deal with the above comments?
b) Suggest how future courses in this area could be improved.
c) Identify three **other areas** of work which are the responsibility of this department.

This question is similar to Question 2, but has the added part on the documents used in the department. A common mistake made by candidates in this type of question is just to give the name of the document and not to explain its use or the type of information it may contain.

The Purchases Department will also have to deal with Invoices, which are a bit like a bill which details what has been bought, the quantity, the price, the date, the VAT and the total owed. It will also show whether any discount has been given.

The key to this question is recognising that Fire Prevention and Evacuation comes under Health and Safety and is therefore the responsibility of the Human Resources Department.

For the second part of the question, you will need to take account of each of the bullet points and identify what was actually wrong and how to improve on this.

a) HR Department
b) For bullet point 1, you could mention that the trainers could try to involve the employees by asking them what they wanted in the course. Bullet point 2 really means making sure that the organisation uses reputable trainers. For bullet point 3, a programme of what is to be delivered should be issued before the course starts, or trainers should be invited to see the employees at work to get a better understanding of what their jobs involve.
c) Any of the following answers will be acceptable: Selection and Recruitment, Grievance, Dismissal, Welfare and Training.

Chapter 2

Office layout

You need to know about

▸ different types of office layout

▸ layouts for different activities

▸ layouts of workstations

▸ appropriate furniture to use.

A pleasant working environment is very important for the health, safety and welfare of all employees. There are two main types of office layout.

a The traditional workspace is usually single rooms – sometimes known as cellular or closed workspace.

b The open-plan office is a more modern idea and usually consists of a large number of employees working in the same big area – probably separated by screens, plants and furniture.

The types of exam questions for this topic tend to focus on the advantages and disadvantages of working in each of these environments, the factors which will affect chosen layouts and how best the furniture and equipment can be arranged for effective and efficient workflow.

More flexible working environments have also led to more flexible working practices, so you will also be expected to describe some common associated terms including hot desking, flexitime, touchdown areas, job-share and carrels.

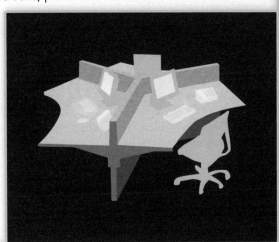

General question 1 –

a) Suggest two advantages an open-plan office layout has over the more traditional closed layout.

Suggestion 1 <u>It is easier for managers to find and supervise</u> <u>employees, as they are all located in the one place and can usually</u> <u>be seen clearly at their desks.</u>

Suggestion 2 <u>Costs can be kept down, both in the space that is</u> <u>taken up by the furniture and equipment and because equipment and</u> <u>resources can be more easily shared.</u>

Knowing the advantages and disadvantages of open-plan and traditional offices is the key to this question. Be careful that you give the advantages of open-plan offices.

b) Explain what is meant by the following terms which can be associated with open-plan offices.

Staff Social/Chill-out Zone

Usually an area within an open-plan office where the staff are permitted to take their breaks and eat, drink and socialise. It will not be too far from their workstations, so they will still have to be considerate to others who may be working around them.

Carrels

Use screens to create little booths where an employee can have a bit more privacy.

Touchdown Areas

Designated points, either at desks or by the coffee bar, where an employee who is hot-desking or teleworking can use their laptop to log into the organisation's network to pick up e-mails and do some work. They are not bookable and are only intended to be used for short periods of time.

Part b) is about knowing the terminology associated with flexible working. Make sure you clearly explain the term and read over your answer to check that it makes sense.

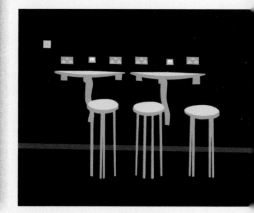

What you need to know at **Credit** **level ...**

In addition to what you need to know at General level, you must be able to

▶ evaluate the different office layouts

▶ discuss the implications of these layouts for management.

Look out for

At Credit level, you will be asked to evaluate different office layouts. You should be able to recommend one type of layout for a given situation. You must always justify your recommendations.

Look out for

Make sure you can explain terms like job-share and flexitime clearly.

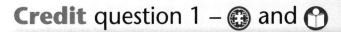

Credit question 1 –  and

Central Office Supplies, located in Perth, have just moved into a new purpose-built flexible workspace. Although they have state-of-the-art equipment and facilities, staff have raised the following issues:

a) 1 The office is too busy at peak times.
   2 Some people can't concentrate, as it is too noisy and they are easily distracted.
   3 The travelling expenses of the Sales Managers are becoming too high, especially those from the Borders and Aberdeen.
   4 Because of reduced car-parking space, some employees are becoming stressed at the time it takes them to find parking when they arrive at work in the morning.
   Suggest how the Office Manager could overcome these problems.

b) Explain the benefits of teleworking to an **employer**.

Part a) of this question has two parts to it. First, you should give a solution and then an explanation.

*Note that the word **employer** has been highlighted, so make sure your answer reflects this. Candidates sometimes confuse whether the answer is for the **employer** or **employee**.*

a) 1 *If the office is too busy at peak times, then it would seem reasonable to offer employees the opportunity to work from home. This would reduce pressure on the facilities.*
   2 *Remind staff that they need to observe some work rules within the work areas. Provide carrels and hot rooms that staff can book for more privacy.*
   3 *Increase the use of videoconferencing, which will allow employees to talk face to face without having to travel, thus reducing costs.*
   4 *Encourage the use of car-sharing, public transport and cycling to work. Provide lockers and showers for cyclists and guaranteed parking spaces for those who car-share.*

b) *Teleworking is the term used to describe when an employee will work away from the office using ICT equipment. The benefits gained by the employer are:*
   • *Less space is needed to accommodate the employees.*
   • *Employees are more motivated, as they can arrange their jobs around their home life.*
   • *The employer can keep good staff who might otherwise have left due to changes in working conditions.*
   • *Teleworking usually leads to a reduction in absenteeism.*

Look out for

Always try to give a different way to solve each problem.

Look out for

Make sure you know the difference between homeworking and teleworking, as these two terms are often confused. You should also know the advantages and disadvantages of each to both the employer and the employee.

Credit question 2 – 📖

a) Jorge da Silva is opening a new branch of his consumer-advice offices and needs to consider the most appropriate layout for the office. Suggest the most suitable layout for him, and justify your answer.

b) Jorge's colleague Frank often works away from the office; recommend two pieces of equipment Frank could use to stay in touch. Give reasons for your recommendations.

You will be expected to explain in your answer to this question that Jorge needs to make the best use of the space he has available. In addition, he needs to choose carefully the furniture he will use and to be aware that on some occasions he may have to speak to his clients in private. Therefore you can choose to write about either a flexible, open-plan office or cellular layout as long as you justify your answer.

In part b), you should be mentioning how ICT has improved communications and has therefore allowed people now to work in the office, at home and while travelling.

a) *The office needs to be flexible to suit the needs of the organisation: an open reception area makes it easier to supervise staff, share equipment and helps to encourage teamwork. However, in order to ensure client confidentiality, a second closed room should be available for face-to-face discussions.*

b) ***A laptop –*** *this could be set up for Wi-Fi and would mean that Frank could have access to the internet and e-mail as long as he is in an area with Wi-Fi.*

A mobile phone – *with this piece of equipment, Frank can call, text, leave voicemail messages, and if necessary take pictures.*

Personal Digital Assistant (PDA) – *also known as a Blackberry or iPhone. These are handheld devices which basically act as mini-PCs and allow the user to e-mail, phone and read documents.*

Safe working practices and procedures

What you need to know at **General** **and** **Credit** **levels ...**

You need to know about

▶ potential hazards

▶ first-aid requirements

▶ display-screen regulations

▶ working environment

▶ emergency and evacuation procedures.

You need to have an awareness of:

▶ the provisions of the main Health and Safety legislation

▶ the responsibilities of the employer and the employee.

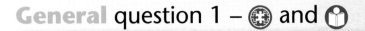

General question 1 – ⊕ and 📖

a) The following incidents have recently occurred in your organisation. Suggest how these problems could be avoided in future.

   i) A member of staff fell over an open filing-cabinet drawer while carrying some boxes.
   The employer needs to reposition the filing cabinets so that they are not in the path of employees. The employee should not be carrying boxes in such a way that they can't see where they are going.

   ii) A member of staff got her scarf caught in the shredding machine as she was destroying some documents.
   The employer should have guards on any dangerous pieces of equipment, and employees should take care when wearing items of jewellery, scarves or any other long or trailing clothing when using the equipment.

b) State three responsibilities of the employee if they witness an accident at work.

   i) *fetch or contact a first-aider*

   ii) *wait with the injured person until help arrives*

   iii) *complete an accident-report form.*

This question is covering the area of maintaining a safe working environment. Both employers and employees have responsibilities in this area. It is the duty of the employer to provide a safe working environment, and it is the duty of the employee to work in a safe manner and not to act in such a way as to be a danger to themselves or others. Employers must minimise the risks to their employees, and employees must report any hazards that exist.

❗ Look out for

Many exam questions will ask about Health and Safety with particular emphasis on the use of ICT – so know about the effects of working at workstations.

General question 2 – and

a) The following incidents occurred within Hobbs & Co. Suggest an appropriate solution to each of the following problems.

   i) When a small fire occurred recently, staff did not know what to do.

   Ensure that regular fire drills are carried out so that staff know what to do in the case of an emergency.

   Ensure that staff are trained in the use of fire extinguishers and other relevant procedures. Display fire-evacuation notices clearly in all public areas.

   ii) Several staff received an electric shock from the printer in the Finance Department.

   Report faulty equipment immediately. Switch off the printer and put up a notice that it is out of order. Call in an engineer. Train staff not to interfere with the equipment. Ensure that all equipment is maintained regularly.

b) Describe **two** actions which should be taken by employers to ensure that **computer operators** work in a safe environment.

Your answers should not repeat any points made in part (a).

1 *Ensure that workstations meet minimum requirements.*

2 *Provide anti-glare screens, wrist guards, foot rests and adjustable chairs.*

*The first part of this question is concerned with **employees** and what they should do with regard to fire precautions and working safely. Notice how the second part of the question is asking about what the **employer** needs to do. Be careful and make sure your answer addresses these points. In part b), pay attention to the words in bold. This is a hint to get you to consider specific issues related to working with ICT equipment.*

Look out for

Know the difference between a Hazard and a Risk.

General question 3 – 🔾 and ✚

a) Explain why it might be a good idea to store an Accident Report Form and a Hazard Report Form on the organisation's intranet.

b) Complete the Accident Report Form from the information given in the following situation.

Akbar Ali from Finance slipped on the stairs at the south end of floor 2 yesterday about 9:40am and badly sprained his ankle. Fortunately, Mark Thomson from Reception, one of the first-aiders, was passing and, although he was able to apply a cold compress, thought it best that Akbar went to the local accident and emergency for a check-up.

To answer the first part of this question, you need to mention that the advantages of storing forms on the intranet is that they can be completed quickly and easily and sent to the correct person. The most up-to-date version will also be used, as the version on the intranet can be changed easily.

Accident Report Form

Name of injured person and Department/Section	*Akbar Ali, Finance*
Date and time of accident	*(yesterday's date) 9:40am*
Brief description of accident	*Akbar slipped and fell on the stairs*
Details of injury	*Badly sprained ankle*
Location of accident	*Stairs at south end of floor 2*
First Aid treatment required	*Cold compress*
Was the injured person taken to hospital/doctor?	*Yes – sent to local A & E*
Names and departments of any witnesses	*Mark Thomson, Reception*
Signature of person reporting the accident	

Date ——————————————

You will be expected to extract the information from the scenario and complete the form, making sure that you don't use the same piece of information twice. You will not be expected to sign the form, but should not lose marks if you do.

Always try to write as neatly and clearly as possible. Use capital letters if you find it easier.

Credit question 1 –

This question is about how employees must avoid potential health hazards by making use of the proper type of facilities available to them. The Health and Safety (Display Screen Equipment) Regulations 1992 outline the employers' and employees' responsibilities.

Sitting at badly designed workstations for long periods can cause health problems. Describe three different health problems associated with this workstation that an operator could suffer from, and for each problem suggest an action that could be taken to overcome it.

Justify your suggestions

1 Sore neck and back because the operator is not sitting on an adjustable chair. Feet are not firmly on the floor.
   Action to overcome this could be to introduce a foot rest and swivel adjustable chair that can properly support the back.
   Justification: If the operator is properly seated there will not be strains on their body which will mean they are less likely to be off work.

2 VDU/monitor is positioned too low (the top of the screen should be on the same level as the operator's eyes), and this will be causing eye strain. Also, with bright sunlight coming in the window from behind, a glare could be affecting the eyes and causing headaches.
   Action to overcome this could be to fit blinds on the window and an anti-glare screen. You could also get a stand for the VDU/monitor, and encourage the operator to take regular breaks from the screen.
   Justification: This will reduce the strain on the eyes and allow the operator to alter conditions to suit themselves and the environment.

3 RSI, or repetitive strain injury, could be a result of not sitting properly and having to stretch for both the keyboard and mouse.
   Action to overcome this could be for the operator to use a wrist guard and tiltable keyboard.
   Justification: All operators are different shapes and sizes so equipment must be adjustable.

Credit question 2 – ⊕

You work in an open-plan office which employs the practices of hot desking and a clear-desk policy. Unfortunately, some staff have recently become quite untidy, leading to a number of potential hazards.

For each of the hazards listed below, recommend a possible solution and **justify** your answer.

 i) Heavy boxes stored on top of filing cabinets
 ii) Used coffee or tea cups and bottles of juice lying beside PCs
 iii) Overloaded power sockets

Again, this question is about recognising what is wrong and being able to make suitable suggestions for changing the situation and making it a safer working environment. The reason the question has mentioned hot desking and clear-desk policy is so that you can refer to what staff should do with food and drink in this type of working environment. Make sure not only that you say what should be done, but also that you say **why** – you will not get full marks if you don't justify your answer.

i) Heavy boxes should be stored at ground level in appropriate storage units. This is to ensure that they will not fall or be dropped on anyone and cause injury.

ii) No food or drink should be consumed anywhere near PCs but only in the designated social areas and chill-out zones. This is to avoid spillages which could ruin the equipment.

iii) Adaptors and more plugs should be purchased, as it is very dangerous to overload sockets: they can fuse, and lost power may mean lost data. Worst still, they can actually overheat and cause a fire.

Reception services

What you need to know at General **level ...**

You need to know about

▌ how the reception should reflect the image of the organisation

▌ reception duties

▌ layouts and features

▌ reporting and dealing with problems

▌ security systems, i.e. swipe cards, CCTV, combination locks and ID.

Reception area

The **reception area** should be bright and welcoming, and the **receptionist** should be friendly and helpful at all times. It may feature pictures and posters, plants, comfortable seats, tea/coffee facilities and toilets. It will also hold **records** – like the staff signing in book, visitors book and appointments diary. Handy phone numbers, such as staff extension numbers, local taxi firms, airports, railway stations and the emergency services should also be available.

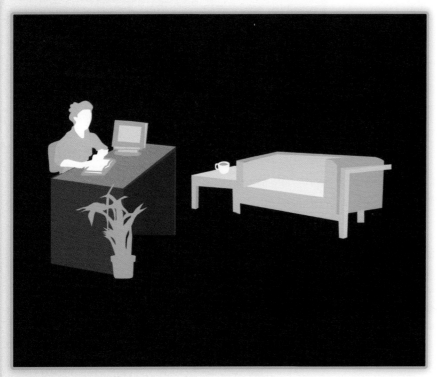

Think safe!

Companies may also use a key pad, combination locks or swipe cards to restrict access. Some organisations have entryphone systems. CCTV is also a popular way of observing and recording details of who is coming and going.

General question 1 –

Paula Simpson is the receptionist at Swift Insurance plc.

Why is it necessary to keep a visitors' book at the reception?
To make sure that reception knows who is in the building and where they are.

All reception areas should have a visitors' book or a reception register to keep details of visitors to the company.

Date	Name	Company	Visiting	Car Registration	Time in	Time out
22 Jan	J Green	Green plc	A Jones, Sales	354 GUS	10.15 am	11.35 am
22 Jan	Alice Brown	PC Components	J Smith, IT		10.30 am	12.10 pm
22 Jan	Anna Schmidt	TR Electrical plc	Jill Gason	ASH 132X	11.45 am	2.10 pm
22 Jan	Peter Andrews	Dewar Graphics plc	Bill Wilson	BDA 354A	3.30 pm	4.45 pm

This information is important because reception needs to know who is in the building in case there is an emergency (like a fire) or in case someone tries to contact the visitor when they are at the company.

Look out for

Questions can ask about the different records kept in reception. It is important that you know what they are and what their purpose is.

General question 2 –

Paula currently uses a paper diary to record details of appointments. She has asked her boss for an electronic diary, as she thinks they are much better.

Give two potential benefits of using an electronic diary.

Benefit 1 *Recurring appointments need only be entered once.*

Benefit 1 *The receptionist can check other people's diaries to find a suitable date/time for a meeting.*

You need to know what facilities you would expect an electronic diary to have so that you can answer this question. There are several – and you only need to give two.

- Regular meetings need only be entered once.
- Appointments cannot easily be double-booked.
- Contact details of staff, taxis, emergency services etc. can be stored in the address book.
- 'To do' or 'task lists' can be generated.
- If networked, the diaries of several people can be checked to find a suitable date/time for a meeting.
- Reminders/alerts can be set on appointments.

Any **two** of the above benefits would be acceptable.

Look out for

You will often be asked to give the benefits/advantages of something (or the disadvantages) in a question. When revising, think about how you would answer a question in both situations. Would you be able to suggest a disadvantage of using an electronic diary?

General question 3 –

Swift Insurance has experienced the following security problems. Suggest a different solution to each of the problems identified.

The visitors' book is not always up to date.

Receptionist should ensure that the visitors' book is always available (ideally open, on top of reception desk, with pen attached).

A new member of staff was refused access to the building.

Reception must be notified of new starts.

A visitor was found in a restricted area.

*All restricted areas should be **locked** – so that only those with a key/swipe card, etc., can enter.*

A member of staff was locked in the building after hours.

Security staff should check the staff in/out book to see if anyone hasn't signed out (and try to contact anyone who seems to be in).

To answer this question successfully, you must be able to suggest a different solution to each problem.

There are several possible solutions, but you only need to suggest one for each problem.

Look out for

Organisations take security very seriously – they don't want their staff or premises to come to any harm. Make sure you know about the basic security precautions that can be taken in a reception area.

General question 4 –

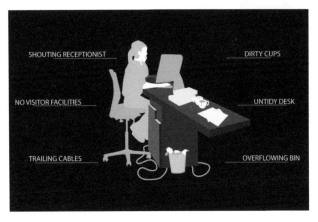

SHOUTING RECEPTIONIST · DIRTY CUPS · NO VISITOR FACILITIES · UNTIDY DESK · TRAILING CABLES · OVERFLOWING BIN

Suggest three features that could improve this reception area.

Feature 1 *comfortable seats for a visitor to wait in*

Feature 2 *a table with refreshments (tea/coffee/biscuits) for visitors*

Feature 3 *tidying the reception area by clearing the desk and emptying the bin.*

You should be able to identify several things that can help make a reception area comfortable for visitors. See page 24 for ideas.

Look out for

Make sure that you suggest three **different** features that could be improved.

General question 5 –

Two customers arrived for an appointment with the Sales Manager at the same time.

Suggest how you could deal with this problem.

Check with the Sales Manager to see when s/he was expecting the

visitors.

If the Sales Manager was not expecting them, you could apologise for

the misunderstanding and offer to arrange another meeting.

Receptionists need to be:

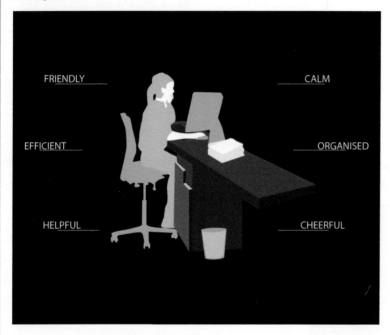

FRIENDLY   CALM

EFFICIENT   ORGANISED

HELPFUL   CHEERFUL

To answer this question successfully, you need to be able to think of a way of resolving the problem without upsetting the customers any further.

You would need to try to find out why the misunderstanding had occurred. You could also check to find out if the Sales Manager had time to see both visitors. If this were possible, you would need to ask the customers if one of them had time to wait.

Look out for

Many questions could have several correct answers. Try to suggest something appropriate for the situation.

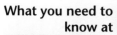

What you need to know at Credit **level ...**

> **In addition to what you need to know at** General level, **you need to know about**
>
> ▶ procedures which organisations may use to deal with security problems.
>
> Typical security problems include
>
> ▶ suspicious parcels/envelopes being left at reception
>
> ▶ angry or aggressive visitors
>
> ▶ members of staff arriving without ID.

Credit question 1 – ⊕

You are a receptionist at Wilson & Jones Kitchens plc. **Suggest** and **justify** an efficient way of dealing with the following situations. Give a *different* suggestion and justification for each.

• A parcel was left at reception when you were refilling the coffee machine. You have no idea who left it or who it is for.
• An angry customer arrives at reception demanding to see the Sales Manager, as the doors have fallen off the kitchen units bought from your company. The Sales Manager is out of town.

Receptionists sometimes have to deal with security issues, and it is important that you know what to do so that you (and others) don't get hurt.

The main things to remember are:
• *stay calm*
• *don't do anything that might put yourself (or others) at risk of injury*
• *contact someone for help (security, or a manager, or the police).*

Suspicious parcel: **Suggestion** – *Do not open or move the parcel.*
     Justification – *You could injure yourself.*
Angry visitor: **Suggestion** – *Contact security/a manager.*
     Justification – *They have been trained to deal with such situations.*

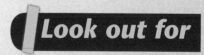 **Look out for**

You could expect to get 1 mark for a correct suggestion and 1 mark for an appropriate justification. **DO NOT** use the same suggestion and justification for both situations.

Mail handling

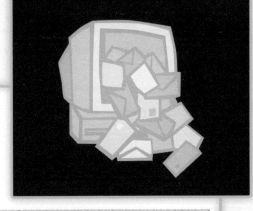

What you need to know at General **level ...**

You need to know about

▷ internal and external mail (including e-mail and fax)

▷ the various methods of sending different types of internal and external mail.

Mail can be transmitted by:

▷ Post	▷ Courier	▷ Private box (PO Box)
The options for post include **first**-or **second**-class post, **courier, recorded, signed for** or **special delivery**	Legal documents or bulky items that need to be delivered quickly	
▷ E-mail	▷ Fax	▷ Voicemail
For communicating with staff and external contacts	When the information is required immediately	This allows a caller to leave a message for the recipient

▷ The main pieces of equipment for dealing with mail include:

▷ **incoming** mail – a date stamp, photocopier, fax and scanner (mail could be scanned onto a computer system and e-mailed to staff – but *don't* scan confidential or private mail)

▷ **outgoing** mail – franking machine, postal scales, addressing machines, folding and inserting machines and labelling machines.

E-mail and fax are often used, and you should know the advantages and disadvantages of both.

	Advantages	**Disadvantages**
E-mail	▷ Efficient, fast and relatively cheap ▷ Files can be attached ▷ One message can be sent to many people at the same time	▷ You need to know the e-mail address you are sending to ▷ The sender needs to request a 'Read Receipt' if they want to be notified when the e-mail is opened ▷ Requires regular checking ▷ Technical difficulties can cause problems
Fax	▷ Speed of transmission – good for urgent information ▷ Relatively low cost	▷ Might take time for message to get from the fax machine to the recipient (centrally located fax) ▷ Sometimes faxed documents are not considered legally binding

Although e-mail is used for a lot of today's mail, the postal service can be useful when

▷ you need to send an actual document	▷ bulky items need to be sent
▷ the intended recipient does not have e-mail	▷ original documents are required, e.g. passport, legal documents, birth certificate

You should be able to suggest the most appropriate methods of sending information.

General question 1 –

Suggest an appropriate method of sending the following mail. Give a different method for each.

A legal contract required by our solicitors in Manchester tomorrow.

Use a courier for the legal contract, to ensure next-day delivery.

An invitation to customers inviting them to a sales event at the end of the month.

Send the invitation to the sales event by post.

Information about the Christmas party for all staff.

Use e-mail for the information on the staff Christmas party.

To answer this question correctly, it is not enough to show that you know different ways of sending information. You must suggest an appropriate way of sending the information in each situation. For example:

- *The legal contract could be sent by either post (special delivery) or courier. Either of these methods would guarantee next-day delivery.*
- *The invitation could be posted (first or second class) or sent by e-mail. There is no great rush, as the event takes place in a few weeks.*
- *The Christmas-party information for staff could be sent by e-mail, posted on the intranet or displayed on posters put on staff notice boards.*

General question 2 –

Jefferson's Employment Agency post paper application forms out to people applying for jobs. They send a lot of forms out each week, and this has become quite costly.

Suggest two other ways that Jefferson's could get forms to people, without having to post them out.

This question wants you to show that you are aware of the relative costs of sending information out. You need to suggest ways that will reduce the postage costs. Provided you use e-mail and have a website, you can make forms available to people without extra postage costs. You could also suggest faxing them – but not everyone has a fax.

Suggestion 1. *Make the application forms available on their website (assuming that they have one).*

Suggestion 2. *Send the forms by e-mail (as an attachment) in response to a request.*

What you need to know at **Credit** level ...

At **Credit** level, you must also be able to give a
▶ justification for your choice of communication method.

Credit question 1 – ✦

Suggest and justify an appropriate method of communication which could have been used in the following circumstances that have arisen recently at Denver and Watkins plc.

• An urgent statement from the Managing Director, received by his assistant at 2:30pm, concerning the takeover of the organisation's coffee shops. The statement had to be in the hands of a national newspaper by 4pm on the same day as it was received.
• An invitation to all customers asking them to attend the launch of a new product in March (in about six weeks' time).
• The next Board meeting is due to take place tomorrow. The Purchasing Director, who is out of the office, has sent a text message to his Personal Assistant asking her to pass on his apologies, as he is unable to attend.
• Notification to all sales representatives cancelling a meeting next week.

You should use a **different method and justification** each time.

Urgent statement

Method	Fax	Justification	The statement has to be received quickly.

Invitation to customers

Method	Mail	Justification	Letters can be personalised – they could be created using mail-merge. The communication is not urgent.

Board-meeting apology

Method	Phone	Justification	Information has to be received fairly quickly. The Personal Assistant would ensure the message gets to the correct person.

Cancelled sales meeting

Method	E-mail	Justification	There is no need for formality.

You would expect to get 1 mark for an appropriate method, and 1 for the justification.

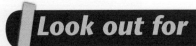

Look out for

Be careful with questions that have several parts like this. Not all methods will be appropriate in each situation. Juggle the methods around as necessary so that you can have a different one for each situation – and a different justification.

Purpose and methods of filing

What you need to know at General **level ...**

You need to know about
- storage and retrieval of information
- alphabetical, numerical and chronological systems
- electronic and manual methods of filing
- when to use different methods.

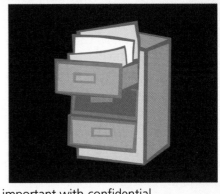

Purpose of filing

Information is filed so that:
- you can find it quickly when it is needed
- the information is held in a safe, secure place – this is particularly important with confidential information
- the documents are kept in good condition
- the organisation meets any legal requirements, e.g. it may be necessary for a school or college to keep exam scripts for a specific period of time.

Methods of filing

Documents can be filed **manually** or **electronically**.

Manual filing means that the documents are stored in filing cabinets, box files and so on. The following classification systems can be used for manual filing:

- Alphabetical
- Numerical
- Chronological

You should know the **main features**, the **advantages** and the **disadvantages** of each system.

Alphabetical	Numerical	Chronological
- Files are arranged in ascending alphabetical order	- Files are arranged in numerical order	- Files are arranged in date order

Advantages - easy to understand - doesn't require an index	**Advantage** - expansion is easy – you just add another file	**Advantage** - most recent correspondence can be found easily
Disadvantages - if an index is used, **training might be required** - **expansion can be tricky** – you might need to shift files from one drawer to another to make room.	**Disadvantages** - it requires an index system and staff may require training in its use. - transposition of file numbers might cause problems.	**Disadvantage** - **never used on its own** – it usually has to be used with another filing system.

continued

Electronic filing means storing files and documents on a computer. Electronic files can be created using software packages, e.g. word-processing, database, spreadsheet and desktop publishing; or you can *scan* documents and store the file created using appropriate software.

Things that you should know about the different types of software used:

▶ the advantages of using the software
▶ the main uses of the software, e.g. database used to store customer records or patient records; spreadsheet used to calculate staff wages or record sales figures.

You also need to know the main **advantages** and **disadvantages** of electronic filing.

General question 1 –

Julie has just started work in the admin office of her local dentist. The patient files have been stored in **chronological** order in the filing cabinet, and staff are wasting a lot of time trying to find patient records.

How could the files be organised better so that files are more easily found?

*This question is about **manual** filing – and the classification systems used with manual filing are **alphabetical, numerical** or **chronological**.*

*In your answer, you just need to suggest **one** method.*

Alphabetical system where the files could be organised by patient surname.

Or

Numerical filing where each patient would be given a patient number and you would use an index to match the number with the patient name.

Look out for

General filing questions that you might be asked about:
- **The purpose of filing** – see previous page.
- **Features of a good filing system** – secure, conveniently located, safe, flexible, appropriate for the type of information being held, quick and simple to use, economical (in terms of set-up, training and running costs).
- **File management** – files and folders have appropriate names, files are stored in the correct folders, out-of-date files are deleted or removed regularly.

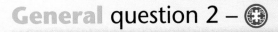

General question 2 –

Central Bank has its head office in Glasgow and branches throughout the rest of Scotland. The bank holds all of its information electronically.

Suggest how each of the following pieces of information could be stored electronically – use a different method for each.
1. Contact information for its customers, e.g. name, address, telephone number
2. A handwritten reference for a new member of staff
3. A letter to a client (or lots of clients) telling them about new bank charges

1 *Database.* Each customer would have their own record. The first name, surname and address would be stored in separate fields (so that you can sort, filter and query the data).

2 *Scanner.* This will produce an image of the document so that it can be stored electronically.

3 *Word-processing software.* A standard letter could be created and then mail-merged with client data to produce personalised letters.

To answer this question, you need to know what you can use different types of software for.

You should be able to give examples of what tasks would be performed using a database, desktop publishing (DTP), spreadsheet and word-processing software. You should also know what a scanner is used for.

Database: Store and manage various records, e.g. employee, customer, student, patient and supplier. It could also be used to manage information on training courses, book company vehicles and so on.

Desktop Publishing: Produce leaflets, newsletters and flyers.

Spreadsheet: Perform calculations and produce graphs for wages, profit/loss figures, departmental budgets, recording sales figures and so on.

Word-processing: Create letters, minutes of meetings, itineraries, memos, reports.

Scanner: Scan documents from hard copy to create an electronic file for storage.

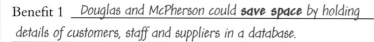

General question 3 –

Douglas and McPherson plc provide catering supplies to many hotels and guest houses across Scotland.

They have been advised that they could improve their efficiency if they used a database to store their data.

Suggest two benefits that using a database could have.

Benefit 1 ___Douglas and McPherson could **save space** by holding details of customers, staff and suppliers in a database.___

Benefit 2 ___They could find customer/supplier, etc., records quickly be **sorting** or **filtering** the data.___

Douglas and McPherson will have a lot of customers – the hotels and guest houses that they sell their goods to.

They will buy the supplies (tea, coffee etc.) from other companies – their suppliers.

They will also have people working for them – their staff. All of this information could be stored in a database.

Other benefits could be:

- They could **query** the database to give reports or specific data, e.g. all the customers in Aberdeen.
- Records can be **inserted** and **deleted** easily.
- Existing records can be **updated** quickly, e.g. customer contact information.
- Customers could be sent personalised letters using mail-merge.

Look out for

Read the question carefully – and give the number of benefits that you are asked for. You should show that you know some of the main features of a database by using terms like **sort, filter, query, insert, delete, update** as appropriate in your answer.

Look out for

This type of question could mention any type of organisation, e.g. a hospital/doctor/dentist (so you will have patients and staff), or a college/school (you will have students, staff, courses), or a solicitor (with clients and staff).

What you need to know at **Credit** level …

In addition to what you need to know at General level, you need to

▶ know the advantages and disadvantages of **centralised** filing and **departmental** filing

▶ know about **integrated software packages**

▶ be able to **evaluate** the different filing methods. When evaluating filing methods, you need to consider **cost, space** and **training**.

To get a good mark at Credit level, you will often be asked to *justify* your answer. This means explaining why you think your answer is the best option.

Problem-solving questions tend to be worth 2 marks each – 1 mark for a *suggestion* on how to solve the problem and another for *justifying* your suggestion.

Credit question 1 –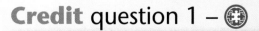

Ali produced a report for his manager highlighting some problems that were being experienced in the office.

The main problems were:

1. Errors made on invoices that are produced using word-processing software – this is at best embarrassing, and at worst costs the company money.
2. All admin staff have access to the payroll data – this information is confidential and should only be accessed by authorised staff in Finance.
3. Letters sent out from the company are laid out differently by each department, and even by individual members of staff within the same department – e.g. with the reference and date in different places, different fonts being used, etc.

His manager has now asked him to *recommend* and *justify* a solution for each of these problems.

Questions often ask you to *justify* or *give reasons for* your answer. As well as suggesting something, you must state why you think it is a good suggestion.

1. **Recommendation:** *Use a spreadsheet to prepare the invoices rather than word-processing software.*
   Justification: *You can enter formulae into the spreadsheet to calculate the value of the invoice – and, as long as the formulae are correct (and data is entered accurately), the invoices will show the right amount.*

2. **Recommendation:** *Password-protect the payroll files so that only those who know the password can view the data.*
   Justification: *Confidential information should be kept secure, and only authorised staff should be able to view it.*

3. **Recommendation:** *Introduce a house style and store a template of it on the company intranet.*
   Justification: *All staff would have access to the same letter template, so all letters produced would be laid out and formatted in the same way.*

Check the number of marks allocated to the questions.

The number of marks will give you a good idea of how many suggestions or reasons you should give when justifying your answers.

Many Credit-level questions that ask for a *suggestion* and *justification* are worth 2 marks – 1 mark for the suggestion and 1 mark for the justification.

Credit question 2 – 📖

The business software on your office PC is fairly old and isn't as easy to use as the software you were trained on at school. You have decided to suggest that the software is upgraded to a newer *integrated software package*. Your boss doesn't know what an integrated software package is!

What is meant by the term *integrated software package*, and how would you justify your suggestion to your boss?

Examples of integrated software packages would be Microsoft Works, Microsoft Office, Lotus SmartSuite or Sun StarOffice. With an integrated package, you really get a suite of programs – typically a word-processing package, spreadsheet, presentation graphics and a database. You won't be asked to name an integrated software package – but you might have used one or more of those listed above. You can usually buy each program separately if you prefer.

An integrated software package is one that allows WP, spreadsheet and database tasks to be carried out using the same suite of programs.

- *The different programs within the suite are easier to learn as they share a common Human–Computer Interface (the instructions are similar across the programs, and the menus, toolbars and screen layout are very similar).*
- *Data can be easily transferred between the packages.*
- *Mail-merge can be carried out within the suite, e.g. using the word-processing program to prepare the letter and the database to store the names and addresses.*
- *It is usually cheaper to buy the integrated suite than it is to buy the packages individually.*
- *More than one package can be open at the same time – making it more efficient to work between/across packages.*
- *Links between files can be easily created, e.g. a link from a report created using the word-processing package to a spreadsheet.*

Credit question 3 – 📖

Your company is considering centralising its filing system and has asked you to identify the potential benefits of a centralised filing system for the next monthly meeting.

What benefits would you identify?

Note that you are being asked for the benefits (or advantages) – not the disadvantages.

*The benefits of anything to an organisation are usually explained in relation to **costs**, **efficient use of space** and **cost-effective use of staff**.*

The costs in this case could be the cost of equipment for filing or the cost of staff to look after the files.

Good use of space could be achieved, as there would be less duplication of equipment throughout the organisation – taking up less space.

The efficiencies could be the result of specialist staff working with the centralised system. They should become very good at their job – naming, storing and retrieving files very quickly.

Potential benefits of a centralised filing system would be:
- *Expert/specialist filing staff would be trained in the filing system – they would be less likely to make errors and should be able to find files easily and efficiently.*
- *Less equipment is required, as equipment is not needed in every department – this would save the organisation money and space.*

If the question had asked for **Disadvantages**, you could have suggested:

- Staff might waste time collecting and returning files.
- The centralised system may not suit all records, e.g. some files might be best stored manually, some electronically. Some might be best using a numerical system, others an alphabetical.

Credit question 4 – ⚙

The following is an extract from the customer database for Highland Organic Foods plc.

Name	Address	Telephone No.	E-mail
Mr Brian Shaw	102 Blackadder Road, Dalbeattie, CA5 9LJ	01556 111222	bshaw @hotmail.com
Mr Alfred Gonzalez	Primrose Cottage, Canonbie, DG3 5GB	08702 634123	gonzalez.a @virgin.net
Miss Qi Wong	West Shore Crescent, Moffat, DG4 3LV	01683 321123	qiwong85 @btinternet.com
Mr Andrew Peterson	14 Baillie Court, Castle Douglas, DG6 9NK	01556 774466	andy.peterson @quista.net
Mrs Morag Smith	31 Grange Road, Edinburgh, EH9 1ZZ	0131 999 1111	msmith31 @hotmail.com
Mrs Shamila Ratna	20 Dunbar Drive, New Abbey, DG9 6YG	08702 101010	shamila @talktalk.net
Miss Fiona McPherson	Heron View, Longtown, CA5 2PP	01228 100200	heronview @hotmail.com
Mr George Wilson	63 Blairwell Drive, Carlisle, CA3 5BL	01228 454545	wilson.g @btinternet. com
Mr Yao Kim	15 Main Road, Dalbeattie, DG9 4QW	01556 332121	yaokim @talktalk.net
Mrs Alice Jefferson	21 Colinton Road, Carlisle, CA3 7XT	01228 991133	alice.jefferson @btinternet.com

Always read the question carefully and answer the question that is asked. If you give the disadvantages, you will waste time – and you won't get any marks for them, even if they are right!

1. Recommend two improvements that could be made to the structure of this database, and justify each one.
2. Pamela Watson, the Sales Manager, needs an alphabetical list of the customer names within each town. Both the Towns and the Surnames should be in ascending order. Having considered how the structure of the database could be improved, suggest how this could be achieved.

1. **Improvement:** Split the name into three fields – Title, first name and surname.
   Justification: This would allow names to be sorted by surname and then first name easily, or for names to be searched for by both first name and surname.
   Improvement: Split the address into three fields – Address, Town and Postcode.
   Justification: This would make it easier to find all the customers in a specific town, e.g. Dalbeattie.
2. The database could be sorted on two fields. The main sort field would be Town, in ascending order, to get the records into order by town, e.g. Canonbie, Carlisle, Castle Douglas, Dalbeattie, Edinburgh, Longtown, Moffat, New Abbey.
   The second sort field would be Surname, in ascending order. The result would be that the customers in each town would then be arranged in ascending order within the town, e.g. within **Carlisle** there would be **Jefferson** followed by **Wilson**.

Look out for

This type of question can be deceiving, as it might look fairly easy. You would probably be able to demonstrate what would be required. But it can be tricky to explain what you would do rather than just do it.

So before the exam, have a good think about what you are **actually** doing when using your software, and practise putting it into words.

Giving an example might help you explain what you mean.

Security of information

What you need to know at General **level …**

You need to know about

- user access
- use of passwords
- care of disks
- back-up procedures.

Companies spend a lot of time and effort trying to protect their data. A lot of what is discussed in this section refers to computerised information – but it is important that manual filing systems are also secure.

All reasonable steps should be taken to ensure that data does not get lost, damaged or corrupted or fall into the wrong hands.

You need to know what things might damage or destroy your computer data. Some things might go wrong by accident, e.g. someone accidentally deletes a file. Other things might be deliberate, e.g. someone steals your computer or sends you a virus.

One common way of trying to protect computer data is to use passwords. Passwords are used to control access to a computer system, to restrict access to a file, to cancel a screensaver or to allow access to an e-mail account.

Password **DOs** and **DON'Ts**	
DO	**DON'T**
Have a mixture of letters and numbers in your password.	Tell anyone what your password is.
Change your password regularly.	Use obvious things like your surname, date of birth, pet's name, star sign, favourite colour etc.
Keep your password secret.	

Also remember

Care of storage media: Floppy disks, CDs and DVDs should be labelled clearly, handled carefully and stored securely in cases or covers away from direct sunlight.

Back-ups: This means having a copy of the data on your computer (maybe on a floppy disk, CD, DVD or memory stick) that you store away from your computer. You could lock it in a filing cabinet, or store it in the company safe. This helps ensure that you still have your data files if your computer is damaged or stolen.

And **ALWAYS** back up regularly, so that the copy is up to date. Many companies will back up their computer systems each night once the staff have gone home.

General question 1 – ⚙

Caledonia Travel plc has recently transferred all its records to an electronic system. The following concerns have been raised by staff:

1 The reception area is in the same room as the computers, and all visitors can see them.
2 All staff have access to all of the company data – including confidential information.
3 Customer bookings were recently lost when a new member of staff accidentally deleted some records.

Provide a **different** solution to **each** of the above problems.

Solution 1 _Ideally, relocate the reception or the computers so that they are in separate rooms_

Solution 2 _Password-protect confidential files so that only those who know the password can access them._

Solution 3 _Back up data regularly so that files can be restored from the back-ups if necessary._

This question is about security of information and controlling access to company data.

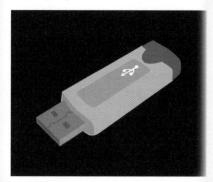

General question 2 – 📖

There have recently been a number of break-ins around Rainbow Paints plc, and the management have asked staff to suggest ways of improving company security.

You have some ideas on how they could improve the **physical security** of their company data and files.

❗ Look out for

Be careful with questions on passwords. It is not usually enough to say 'use a password'. You must relate the use of the password to the question.

So, you would *use a password to …*

* restrict access to the computer
* control access to confidential files
* lock the screensaver until the password was entered
* restrict access to e-mail.

Suggest three things that they could do to restrict access to the company computers and files.

Suggestion 1 *Provide staff with individual log ins*

Suggestion 2 *Password protect files*

Suggestion 3 *Locked offices and PIN entry systems*

This question is about the physical security of data. So, you would want to suggest things that would either
- *restrict/control access to the building and offices, and in particular the areas where the computers are, or*
- *restrict/control access to the company files.*

You could also suggest that
- *an entry system was put on the front door to the company, and staff had to use a PIN (personal identification number) to get in*
- *staff had to sign in at reception*
- *offices were kept locked*
- *entry systems were used on offices, e.g. staff would enter a PIN to unlock the office door or the door to the floor where they work.*

What you need to know at Credit **level ...**

In addition to what you need to know at General level**, you need to know about**

▶ the Data Protection Act 1998.

Look out for

Questions on protecting computers and the data held on them might be about the **physical** protection (where you can lock the computer or data away, or restrict access to the areas where the computers are) or **electronic** protection (using passwords to protect the computer/ computer files).

Credit question 1 –

> Data-users holding information on individuals must comply with the principles of the Data Protection Act. Outline three of these principles.

Look out for

Watch for questions that say 'Outline'. Give a brief explanation of what you mean – don't just list three principles.

There are eight principles in the Data Protection Act. These are:

1. **Data must be obtained lawfully.**
   This means collected from an application form/order form – and the person knows that you are collecting their data and why.

2. **Data must not be held for longer than is necessary.**
   If the data is no longer required, it should be deleted.

3. **Data must be kept secure.**
   This means locked in a filing cabinet, or password-protected on a computerised system.

4. **Data should be accurate.**
   Care should be taken that the data you hold is correct.

5. **Data must be kept up to date.**
   The data should be updated as necessary as time goes on.

6. **Data subjects have the right to see the information held on them.**
   The person whose data you hold has a right to ask to see the information you hold on them. This should be permitted within a reasonable period of time, and it should not cost them much (if anything) to do so.

7. **Data-users must change information if it is incorrect.**
   If the information you hold is incorrect, the data subject can ask that you change it.

8. **Data must only be held for a specific purpose.**
   In a school, records are held to record your attendance and performance; in a bank, records are there to manage your financial transactions with them; in a doctor's practice, the data is held for medical purposes.

So, you could choose any three from the eight.

Equipment – features and uses

What you need to know at General **level ...**

You need to know about features of different pieces of equipment and software.

For example:

▶ photocopier

▶ laminator

▶ binder

▶ scanner

▶ DTP

▶ printers.

You also need to be able to choose the most appropriate piece of equipment for different types of jobs.

Reprography is the name given to the process of duplicating and copying documents. To most people this usually means photocopying; however, it is important to remember that a Reprographics Department will have responsibility for providing a service to the organisation, which will mean that, in addition to making copies, it will also be responsible for the collation, binding and presentation of these copies.

General question 1 –

Identify each piece of equipment and describe two features and two tasks it will perform.

Equipment
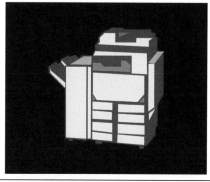 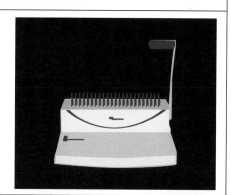
 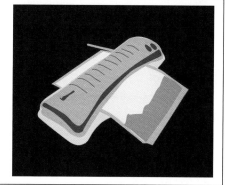

This is a suggested solution.

	Features	Tasks
	Can copy many different types of documents.	Prepare copies of policies and procedures.
	Can copy in colour, double-sided and staple.	Travel Expense Claims and other forms.
	Collates pages of booklets together.	Binds reports for use at meetings.
	Adds professional-looking covers.	Provides strong booklets that may be used regularly, e.g. Health and Safety policy.
	Takes an exact copy of a document, picture or graphic.	Scans copies of incoming mail and saves them electronically to reduce storage space.
	Allows for scanned images to be uploaded to an intranet.	Scans pictures to put into brochures.
	Uses heat to melt a plastic coating around a document to protect it from wear and tear.	Can be used to create visitor passes.
	Also allows the document to be kept clean if it is used in an area where it can attract grease or dirt, e.g. in a kitchen.	To protect notices displayed in public areas.

When answering this question, you would be expected to identify the piece of equipment. Then state two separate features of each piece and give two different uses for each piece. You must clearly make differences between the features and the uses to gain marks. When you are asked to identify from pictures, take time to examine the picture carefully, as it is easy to confuse the lesser-known machines like binders and laminators.

Look out for

Be careful not to use the name of the piece of equipment when describing what it does. For example, don't say a binder binds or a scanner scans – you will not get marks for this. Suggest different tasks that each piece of equipment could be used for.

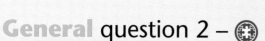

General question 2 – ✳

You are the Administrative Assistant in the publicity department of a major hotel chain. Suggest the most appropriate equipment and software to be used in each of the following situations.

a) Preparing menus for use in the restaurant and bar

b) Preparing advertising leaflets for the hotel which include photos and diagrams

a) Item of equipment

*The number of copies required will not be large, so an **inkjet printer** would be cheaper than a laser for this type of job.*

Item of software

*The menu is mainly text, and is something which could change on a daily basis, so would most probably be best prepared using **word-processing software**.*

b) Item of equipment

*The best software for the advertising leaflets would be a **desktop publishing** program which allows for the placement of text and graphics in more complicated layouts.*

Item of software   *The leaflets could be printed using a **laser printer** which can do larger runs and produce good-quality black-and-white and colour copies.*

*This question has a different emphasis from the previous one. You are expected to be able to identify the piece of **equipment** most suited to the job and what **software** would be the most effective.*

Look out for

Try to ensure that you don't use the same piece of equipment or software twice in your answer – you will be expected to know a variety.

General question 3 – ⚙

Catriona Forbes is the chairperson of the Eco Committee in her school and has been asked to produce a newsletter to update staff and pupils on the progress towards the next green flag. She hopes to be able to produce this newsletter on a monthly basis.

a) Advise Catriona on one item of software and one item of equipment she could use to produce the newsletter. You must also state clearly one advantage of each.

Item of software _Desktop publishing software where you can use a newsletter template. Alternatively, you could also use word-processing software which allows text to be displayed in columns and photos and graphics to be easily inserted._

Advantage _DTP software has predetermined layouts and provides tools which make it easy to use graphics and pictures and other design-enhancement features. Word-processing software is easy to use and also has features which can make a newsletter attractive._

Item of equipment _A computer will need to be used if the newsletter is produced electronically, but other pieces of equipment, e.g. scanner, digital camera, printer etc. could be mentioned – though the advantage you give must be appropriate to the piece of equipment._

Advantage _Using a computer can save previous editions of newsletter._

This is a very open question, as any appropriate piece of software mentioned with a suitable advantage could be accepted. It would also be fair to say that the same applies to the piece of equipment. The best answer would be to use the 'keyword' in the question, which is 'newsletter', and try to think about what would be used to produce this in a school situation.

What you need to know at Credit level ...

In addition to what you need to know at General level, you should be able to discuss

▶ the effects of equipment selection, e.g. staff training required

▶ in-house copying versus external agencies.

Very often, the reprographics function is centralised to improve efficiency. This will mean that the staff working in this area need to be very skilled and must receive training so that they can:

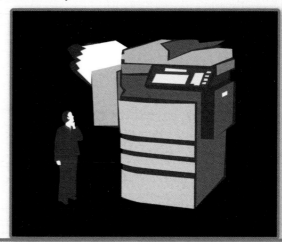

▶ operate the equipment for maximum efficiency

▶ trace faults and take follow-up action if necessary

▶ have an awareness of the legislation which affects copying, e.g. copyright.

It is important that training is relevant and targets the needs and requirements of the staff. Training should also be offered regularly and be carried out by properly qualified instructors. Even with a good Reprographics Department, there will be times when an organisation may arrange to have its copying done by an external agency or *outsource* this work in order to take advantage of greater expertise or savings.

Credit question 1

a) Gemma Higgins is the Reprographics Manager of Claret plc. Reprographics Assistants have experienced the following problems:
  (i) They are unsure what to do when equipment breaks down.
  (ii) They do not know how to use a new piece of equipment.

What advice should Gemma give to Reprographics Assistants to prevent these problems from recurring? Justify your answers. Give a different answer to each problem.

The answer to part a) of this question focuses on staff training. You will be expected to say that staff should know how to use equipment properly, and know what to do when it breaks down giving reasons for what you said.

i) They would be expected to switch off the item; place a sign telling people not to use it; report breakdowns; provide extra training on Health and Safety.
 Justification: to ensure item fixed properly; to ensure no-one uses broken equipment; to ensure safety of employees so that no-one gets hurt in future.
ii) State that staff should not be using any equipment until they have been properly trained.
 Justification: This is for their own safety and to make sure that they don't do any damage. In addition to training, staff should know the procedures and have a step-by-step guide which they can refer to when necessary.

Look out for

Always read a question fully before attempting to answer it; check out the keywords, i.e. 'suggest, justify, describe'. Then read over your answer to make sure it makes sense.

b) Suggest two advantages to an organisation of outsourcing/using an external agency for reprographics work.

Outsourcing is when an organisation chooses to contract work out. They may do this for a variety of reasons, usually to save money.

b) *Experts in this area will have better equipment and be able to produce a job more quickly and to a better degree of quality and presentation.*

This leaves the employees within the organisation more time to spend on their own duties rather than on copying.

Avoids company expenditure on keeping up to date with the right equipment or machine maintenance.

Credit question 2 –

Rebecca Smith works in an exclusive beauty-therapy salon and has been given the task of producing a new brochure for clients showing the treatments available and the costs. Her manager is keen that this brochure should be of the highest standard, as it will reflect on the image of the salon if it is not well produced.

Rebecca is unsure whether to produce this brochure herself or use an outside agency.

Recommend which method would be best, and **justify** your answers.

The brochure should be produced by the outside agency. This is because they would have access to specialist staff, better equipment, design facilities and would produce a higher quality finish.

This question, like the previous one, mentions 'outsourcing', but the emphasis is slightly different, as you are expected to make a recommendation of which method would be best. This means that either method would be an acceptable answer as long as you give reasons, i.e. justify why you have made this choice. Therefore you could say:

*Rebecca could produce the leaflet **in house** and easily make a very good brochure using desktop publishing software and a colour laser printer. It would be a cheaper option, could be geared to exactly what the salon wants and may even be done more quickly than if it was outsourced.*

*However, if an **outside agency** is chosen, then they will probably be able to produce a much better-quality result. They will have specialist design staff who will be able to give the brochure that special look. They may also have access to better equipment, e.g. digital cameras and software. It will also mean that Rebecca can continue with her daily duties without having to worry about the brochure.*

Look out for

If you decided to compare the different methods, this would also be acceptable as long as you made clear in the end which option you were going to **recommend**.

Look out for

Always try to make your answers relevant to the scenario; you need to give specific facts in your answer that match the question.

Credit question 3 –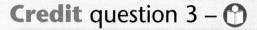

a) Besides photocopying, describe two other tasks that would be carried out by a Reprographics Assistant.

b) Justify why a Reprographics Assistant should be familiar with both the Copyright, Designs and Patents Act and the Health and Safety at Work Act.

a) A Reprographics Assistant may be responsible for using the binding machine to add covers to reports or other documents or using a digital camera to take photographs required, then downloading them for editing.

b) **Copyright, Designs and Patents Act 1988**

A Reprographics Assistant should know that it is illegal to copy text from books, magazines, newspapers or other publications without permission from the authors, and staff using photocopiers need to be aware of the limitations that exist on the number of copies that they can make in some circumstances.

Health and Safety at Work Act 1974

Reprographic Assistants must be aware of the potential dangers of working with the equipment they have been trained to use. They should be familiar with any procedures that need to be followed – for example, if the machine breaks down or there is a paper jam.

The emphasis in this question is to make sure you understand that reprographics is the name given to the section or department that will support the copying process in an organisation. This means that it will perform a whole range of other tasks including printing, binding, laminating, collating, scanning and designing.

The second part of the question is more difficult. It is really testing another area of the syllabus, as you will be expected to know the purpose and content of both of the acts mentioned and how they can **specifically** relate to the job of the Reprographics Assistant.

People-based, paper-based and electronic

What you need to
know at **General** level ...

You need to know about

◗ identifying, accessing and extracting information

◗ interpreting information.

The three main sources of information are:

◗ people-based

◗ paper-based

◗ electronic.

People-based

◗ face-to-face meetings

◗ telephone conversations

◗ a quick way of passing on information

◗ no written record of what has been said

◗ as it isn't written down, it might be forgotten or misinterpreted.

Paper-based

◗ reference books (dictionary or thesaurus)

◗ leaflets

◗ brochures

◗ directories

◗ timetables (for trains and buses)

◗ catalogues

◗ posters

◗ letters

◗ reports

◗ maps and all kinds of files!

Anything that is printed is paper-based.

For the exam, it is important that you can **name** the main paper-based sources. You should also be able to say what each source would be **used** for.

Paper-based sources are handy if there is no internet access or if the internet is unavailable for technical reasons.

Reading a magazine, newspaper or brochure can also be fun!

Electronic

◗ the internet

◗ company intranet

◗ information in databases, spreadsheets or on teletext.

◗ CD-ROMs (often used for telephone directories and encyclopedias – but, just like printed sources, they can go out of date quickly).

The first place that most people go to for information is the internet. The internet is also used for e-commerce – buying and selling goods.

General question 1 –

Describe one advantage and one disadvantage of using the internet as a source of information.

Advantage *Provided the website is well maintained, the information will be up to date.*

Disadvantage *Technical problems could mean that the information is unavailable.*

! Look out for

Give different suggestions. Don't say that an advantage would be that the information was up to date and then suggest that a disadvantage is that the website might be out of date.

The main advantages are:
- *available 24/7*
- *up to date*
- *lots of information – perhaps with video clips and sound too*
- *often instant – great when checking flights or hotel accommodation, as you can get feedback on availability and price straight away*
- *you can book and pay online (using a debit or credit card)*
- *search engines can help you find the information you need – even if you don't have a web address/URL.*

Problems (disadvantages):
- *a website might be out of date*
- *you can't always be sure that the information on a website is accurate*
- *possible technical problems.*

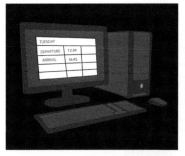

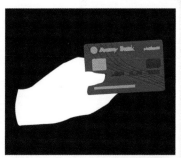

General question 2 – ⊛

> **Funky Dance and Fitness Centre** has a website where it advertises its classes and events.
>
> Members and clients have raised the following concerns:
> 1. They can't easily find what they are looking for on the website.
> 2. There is no way of asking questions if something isn't clear.
> 3. They have to phone or visit the centre if they want to buy merchandise, e.g. Funky Dance T-shirts and sweatshirts, dance trousers, posters and so on.
>
> Suggest a different solution to each of the problems identified above.
>
> Suggestion 1 _Add a contents list on the Home Page._
>
> Suggestion 2 _Add an FAQ (Frequently Asked Questions) section._
>
> Suggestion 3 _Add an online order form._

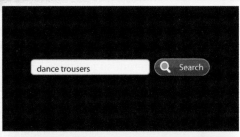

Navigation aids:

- *contents list*
- *search facility*
- *hyperlinks*
- *clear and easy to understand pages*

To provide answers to questions:

- *FAQ (frequently asked questions)*
- *e-mail facility*
- *contact information clearly displayed*

To allow people to buy online:
- *introduce an e-commerce facility*
- *add an online order form*
- *remove out-of-date products*

⚠ Look out for

Be careful if you mention a search facility within the website – you must make it clear that you mean **within the website** and must not confuse it with a search engine like Google or Yahoo.

General question 3 – 📖

Name and explain two features of websites which make them user-friendly.

Feature 1 _Hyperlinks – provide links to make it easy for users to visit other pages or sites._

Feature 2 _Graphics – to let customers see what a product looks like to help them decide whether or not they want to buy._

*With this question, you would probably get 4 marks: 1 mark for **naming** a feature and another for **explaining** what the feature is.*

So, you could choose any two from the table below.

Feature	Explanation
Hyperlink	Redirects (or links) users to another web page or website. CLICK HERE TO SEARCH FOR A CLASS
Hotspot	A special area on the screen, sometimes used as a hyperlink. It could change its appearance, i.e. if it is a picture, the picture might change, or it could play a sound when clicked, or the cursor changes to a hand.
Search facility	Searches *within* the website to allow visitors to find what they are looking for quickly » SEARCH [ ] OK Search by brand ▼
E-commerce	This allows users to purchase goods and services online.
FAQ section	Displays a list of regularly asked questions and their answers. Users will often find in the FAQs the answer to a question that they have.
Graphics	Used to show customers what products look like, e.g. merchandise sold by Funky Dance and Fitness Centre.
Secure site	Secure sites are often used in e-commerce so a customer can pay for goods online in a secure, risk-free link to the company. The lock on the Status bar indicates that a site is secure.

General question 4

You sometimes get short 1-mark questions on sources of information. These can be tucked away in questions that draw on the content from different sections of the syllabus.

The questions on this page are the type that you might find cropping up for the odd mark here and there.

Many customers do not know that **Funky Dance and Fitness Centre** has a website.

How could this problem be solved?

- *Advertise it on flyers, posters, stationery and other websites,*
  or
- *Set up links to it from other websites.*

How would you explain the meaning of the term Hyperlink?

Text or graphic which you click to be directed to take you to another web page/site, or to a file, picture, program, film, sound file etc.

» PAYMENT METHODS

What does the term e-commerce mean?

Selling and buying goods online.

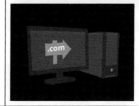

Give one disadvantage of people-based information.

Conversations can be forgotten, or misinterpreted, unless they are written down.

Suggest one disadvantage of paper-based information.

- *Paper-based information can go out of date quickly,*
  or
- *It can be expensive to produce and distribute.*

What you need to know at Credit level

You don't need to know any additional content for the Credit level exam.

However, the questions asked will be more in-depth and will require fuller answers.

Remember your keywords – you may be asked to *justify* or *recommend* a solution or course of action.

When you *justify* something, you must suggest an answer *and say why you think it is a good thing or a bad thing.*

You need to know what an intranet is before you can answer this question.

- *An intranet is a computer network that is **internal** to a company.*
- *It is used to share information within the organisation.*
- *It can only be accessed by employees of the company.*

You can then suggest the types of things that an organisation could use it for.

Credit question 1 – 🎲

Identify the uses of an intranet to an organisation.

Uses of an intranet to an organisation:
- *Allows staff to access shared software applications.*
- *Allows staff to access organisational policies online such as Health and Safety guidelines, evacuation procedures, accidents-at-work procedures etc.*
- *Allows information to be immediately available on staff desktops.*
- *Company policies, etc., can be updated centrally.*
- *Internal e-mail communication is possible.*
- *Can control access to the internet.*

Look out for

Always check the number of marks allocated to a question. This will give you an idea of how many different points you need to make.

If the above question was worth 2 marks, any two of the suggestions would be enough.

Credit question 2 – 🎲

Your boss thinks that the company should introduce an intranet.

Suggest two ways in which she could justify the introduction of an intranet to the other managers.

The introduction of an intranet could be justified as
- *costs of printing and photocopying would be reduced, and*
- *communications between staff would be quicker and cheaper.*

*To **justify** the introduction of an intranet, you would need to identify the potential benefits to the organisation. Potential benefits of an intranet to an organisation:*

 Reduces cost of: purchasing software, photocopying, printing.

 Helps communicate information on: work and non-work related matters, e.g. telephone extension numbers, internal job vacancies, staff social events.

 Speeds up communication as: policies and documents can be updated online, staff can access files immediaely.

Credit question 3 –

Give two potential uses of the internet by the HR Department when recruiting staff. **Justify** your suggestions.

The Human Resources department could use the internet to:

i) Advertise job vacancies.
   Justification: It would be possible to reach a wide range of potential employees. Or you could suggest that anyone looking for a job could find out what jobs you had available at a time that suited them – 24/7.

ii) Put application forms online.
   Justification: Potential employees could obtain an application form without having to contact the company direct, and this would save the company money as it means it doesn't have to print the forms out and post them to people.

In this question, the department you have to consider is the Human Resources Department. When recruiting staff, they need to:
- advertise the job
- send out application forms to people who want to apply
- tell people who a bit about what the company is like as an employer.

Look out for

Any of the questions asked in the exam could be linked to a department or a job role that you should know about. So, make sure you know what kinds of things go on in the main functional departments, e.g. Sales, Purchasing, Human Resources, Finance and Marketing. You should also be able to say what tasks are carried out in some of the key job roles in each area. What would the Admin Assistant in Purchasing do – or in Sales or HR? What would the Purchasing Manager – or Sales or HR Manager – do?

Credit question 4 –

Your company has recently decided to set up an e-commerce facility on the internet.

Give two examples of how they might justify such a decision
- to the **Sales** Department

  or
- to the **Purchasing** Department.

The company could justify its decision to the **Sales** Department by pointing out that it would

- give the sales team a larger customer base (which would potentially increase sales)
- allow the company to offer internet discounts (which would encourage potential customers to buy things from us).

The company could justify its decision to the **Purchasing** Department by pointing out that it would

- allow them to purchase goods at a time that suits them – 24/7
- be easier for them to compare the prices of different suppliers and help them to find the best deal.

The main potential benefits to a Sales Department would be:

- Larger **customer** base
- Goods can be **sold** (to anywhere) 24/7
- Orders can be placed (and paid for) with immediate confirmation online
- Reduces admin costs
- Allows the company to offer customers internet discounts.

The main potential benefits to a Purchasing Department would be:

- Access to a larger **supplier** base
- Goods can be **purchased** (from anywhere) 24/7
- Orders can be placed **by us**, with immediate confirmation online
- Reduces admin costs
- Can benefit from internet discounts and special internet prices
- Easier to compare prices from different suppliers.

Look out for

Some exam questions might ask for an answer that would be targeted to a particular department, e.g. Sales or Purchasing in this question. So, make sure that you know the differences between them.

Credit question 5 –

Identify and describe two ways in which an organisation might use the internet for business purposes.

An organisation could use the internet to advertise the products that it sells.
This usually means putting pictures of the products on the internet, with a description of the product and the price. Details of any terms and conditions of purchase may also be given.
An organisation could also use the internet to make travel arrangements.
Staff could research plane, train and ferry timetables, compare prices, book and pay for tickets and accommodation online and print out e-tickets.

You should be able to think of several things that companies use the internet for, e.g.

- advertise their products
- e-mail staff and customers
- make travel arrangements
- check competitors' products and prices
- recruit staff
- e-commerce.

To answer this question fully, it is not enough to identify the ways it can be used – you have to go on to describe what they mean.

Credit question 6 –

Sources of information can be people-based, paper-based or electronic.

Identify and describe one disadvantage of each.

Justify your suggestion.

People-based: A disadvantage is that what was said could be forgotten or misinterpreted.

Justification: This could result in someone taking the wrong course of action/making the wrong decision.

Paper-based: A disadvantage is that it goes out of date quickly.

Justification: By the time a document is prepared, copied and distributed, the information that it contains could no longer be accurate.

Electronic: A disadvantage is that you can't always be sure that what you find on websites is correct.

Justification: Anyone can create a website and put information on it – so you need to try to ensure that the website that you are using is reliable.

Look out for

You could also be asked a question that asks you to identify and justify the *advantages* of each – so have answers ready for that too!

The main disadvantages of the different sources are:

People-based
- There is no written record of what has been said.
- It's easy to forget what has been said, or to misinterpret something.

Printed
- It goes out of date quickly.
- It's expensive to produce and distribute.

Electronic
- What you read on a website might not be up to date.
- It might not be accurate.
- There could be a technical problem resulting in the website being unavailable.

Chapter 6

Equipment, software and forms

What you need to know at **General** **level ...**

You need to know about different types of presentation:

◗ charts and graphs

◗ forms

◗ memos

◗ itineraries.

You also need to know about different software and equipment that can be used to prepare and give presentations.

Presentation method	Main points
Charts and graphs	◗ used to present statistical and numerical data ◗ usually produced using spreadsheet software ◗ good for showing trends in the data, e.g. sales increasing or membership numbers falling over time ◗ useful when you need to compare one set of figures with another, e.g. sales made each month, or number of pupils in the school each year.
Forms	You should be aware of the purpose of a range of forms: ◗ accident reports ◗ travel and accommodation request forms ◗ fax cover sheets ◗ expenses claims. You should know how to fill out the forms mentioned above.
Memos	These are used to communicate with other employees within the organisation. They can be ◗ completed by hand ◗ completed on a word-processor ◗ delivered by internal e-mail ◗ sent by the internal mail service.
Itineraries	A form used on business trips. It will include details of: ◗ transport arrangements (including plane/train/ferry times) ◗ accommodation details (name, address and telephone number of hotel and details of the booking, e.g. single room, en-suite, with breakfast) ◗ details of meetings – time, place, who the meeting is with and what papers etc. should be taken to the meeting.

question 1 –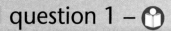

Funky Dance and Fitness Centre is the best place in town for fun, exercise and gigs. Its popularity has grown in recent years, and the Marketing Director prepared this graph to show income from different areas of the business.

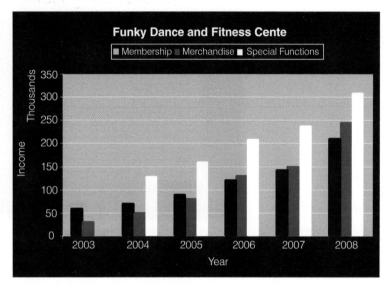

Suggest one reason why a column chart was used to show this information.
It's good for showing trends in the data.

Suggest one other way this information could have been displayed effectively.
A line graph.

Any **one** of the suggestions given on the previous page would be a good reason for using the column chart and would be a good suggestion to make for the first part of the question.

The main reasons for presenting statistical information in a graph are that:
• you can see the information at a glance
• you can spot trends easily, as it is clear which figures are going up or down
• charts are usually easier to read and understand than a table full of figures.

Look out for

This type of question is checking that you know about the different types of **graph/chart** that could be used.

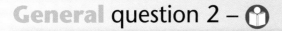

General question 2 –

Peter Green is the Marketing Manager with West Highland College. He presented the following figures at a meeting recently, showing details of student numbers by department over the past few years.

	2005	2006	2007	2008
Business Administration	1200	1325	1100	1240
IT and Web Design	1400	1650	1725	1790
Applied Science	950	1200	1105	1320
Modern Languages	400	320	385	410
Performing Arts	1400	1540	1850	2200
Hospitality and Tourism	1280	1100	1430	1310

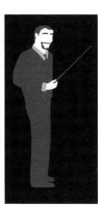

Suggest and describe **two** ways in which Peter could have enhanced his presentation.

(Your answer should refer to equipment/software.)

Suggestion 1 *Presentation software*

Describe how *He could add animation effects/sound/colour/video to enhance the presentation.*

Suggestion 2 *Data projector*

Describe how *He could enlarge the image on the screen so that everyone could see it clearly.*

You need to show that you know what types of equipment and/or software can be used in presentations to answer this question.

Equipment could be a data projector or an interactive whiteboard.

Software could be presentation software (e.g. PowerPoint), DTP, word-processing or spreadsheet.

Use the correct terminology in this type of question. If you mention software, state the type, e.g. spreadsheet or presentation, and *not* the name of the application, e.g. Excel or PowerPoint.

General question 3 –

Amir Halik is the Sales Manager for Web Design International, based in Dundee. He has recently attended a two-day exhibition in Manchester and has his Expense Claim Form to complete.

Study the information below, and then complete the Expense Claim Form for Amir.

Melville Grange Hotel 63 Western Road MANCHESTER M2 4TT		
Amir Halik	Account No. 3311	Room 214
Date	Details	Cost
23/09	Bed & Breakfast Dinner Bar Bill	£85.00 £21.00 £5.75
24/09	Bed & Breakfast Dinner Bar Bill	£85.00 £19.00 £4.25
Total Bill VAT @ 17.5% included		**£220.00**

| **FLYRIGHT**
Edinburgh – Manchester
Return
23/9 – 25/9
Received with thanks
£260.00 | **EASTCOAST RAIL**
Dundee – Edinburgh
Return
23/9 – 25/9
Received with thanks
£33.00 | BRUCE'S TAXIS RECEIPT
23/9
£5.25

BRUCE'S TAXIS RECEIPT
25/9
£5.25 |

The form has been started for you.

(You would complete the form by adding detail to the areas that are shaded.)

Web Design International
Expense Claim Form

| Name | Amir Halik | |
| Department | Sales | |

Person making claim

Dates 23/09 – 25/09	Total Expenditure	

TRAVEL (please give details)	£	p
Return flight (Edinburgh – Manchester)		
Outward – 23/09 Return – 25/09	260	00
Return rail fare (Dundee – Edinburgh)		
Outward – 23/09 Return – 25/09	33	00
Taxi – 23/09	5	25
Taxi – 25/09	5	25

Airfare with Flyright

Eastcoast Rail

2 trips with Bruce's Taxis

ACCOMMODATION (please give details)		
Bed and Breakfast (Melville Grange Hotel)		
23/09 and 24/09	170	00

£85.00 each night

MEALS (please give details)		
Dinner – 23/09 (Melville Grange Hotel)	21	00
Dinner – 24/09 (Melville Grange Hotel)	19	00

Dinner at the hotel for 2 nights

OTHER EXPENSES (please give details)		
Bar Bill 23/09	5	75
Bar Bill 24/09	4	25

Bar bill for 2 nights

TOTAL EXPENSES DUE	523	50

Add them all together to get the total

Employee's Signature Amir Halik	Date 1/10/09

Look out for

Remember to give the details of where the expense has come from. And don't claim for anything that isn't on a receipt.

 question 4 –

Poster Paints plc uses a range of communication methods including e-mail and memos.

What is a memo?

*A memo is a form that is sometimes used for **internal** communication. It has space on it so that you can say who it is to, who it is from and what it is about, and put the date it was sent.*

Describe two ways in which a memo can be completed.

1 *Using **word-processing software***

2 *It can be **handwritten***

Describe two ways in which a memo could be distributed.

1 *Using **internal e-mail***

2 *Using the **internal mail service***

You need to know what a memo is to answer this question – and saying that it is a **form** just isn't good enough to get the marks!

*A memo is a form that is sometimes used for **internal** communication*

- *It has space on it so that you can say who it is to, who it is from, what it is about and put the date it was sent.*

- *A memo can be completed using word-processing software or it can be handwritten.*

- *It can be distributed by **internal e-mail** or it could be delivered using the **internal mail service**.*

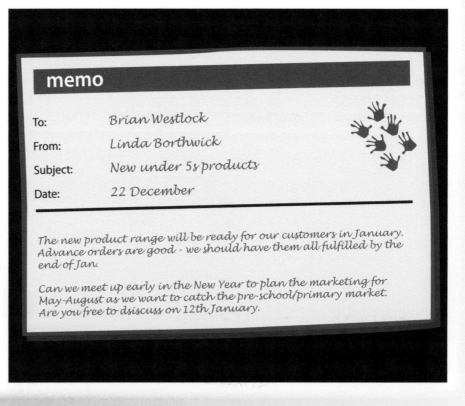

memo

To: Brian Westlock

From: Linda Borthwick

Subject: New under 5s products

Date: 22 December

The new product range will be ready for our customers in January. Advance orders are good - we should have them all fulfilled by the end of Jan.

Can we meet up early in the New Year to plan the marketing for May-August as we want to catch the pre-school/primary market. Are you free to dsiscuss on 12th January.

Reports

What you need to know at  **Credit level ...**

You need to know about

▶ Reports.

Reports can by used to

▶ explain the course of action taken by the company, e.g. a report explaining why the company has decided to centralise its admin services

▶ present a solution to a problem that has been identified, e.g. a security issue

▶ outline and explain a new procedure that is being implemented

▶ present information on how well (or badly) the company has been doing over a period of time, e.g. the Annual Report.

Reports are produced using word-processing software. They should look professional and well laid out – especially if they are going to be read by people outside the organisation.

A report should

▶ be formatted consistently throughout

▶ be checked carefully for spelling, grammar and punctuation errors

▶ incorporate relevant graphics, e.g. pictures, graphs, tables, diagrams, to help clarify what is being reported.

Credit question 1 – ✦

Gill Thomson is the manager at the local Leisure Centre. She holds meetings regularly with her team to keep them up to date with attendance figures at the centre. Gill records this data into a spreadsheet – and uses a data projector to present the spreadsheet to her team at their meetings.

	A	B	C	D	E	F	G
1	Caledonia Leisure Centre – Attendance figures						
2							
3		January	February	March	April	May	June
4	Adult	260	2250	2524	2650	2780	2900
5	Child	5250	5260	5800	5675	5900	6010
6	Concession	2900	2800	3000	3250	4250	4600

Suggest two other ways in which Gill could present this data to her staff, and justify your suggestions.

i) **Suggestion:** *Bar graph*
   Justification: *They are good for showing how one set of data compares with another, e.g. how the number of children attending compares with the number of adults.*

ii) **Suggestion:** *Line graph*
   Justification: *They are good for showing how a set of data goes up and down over a period of time, e.g. numbers of adults, children.*

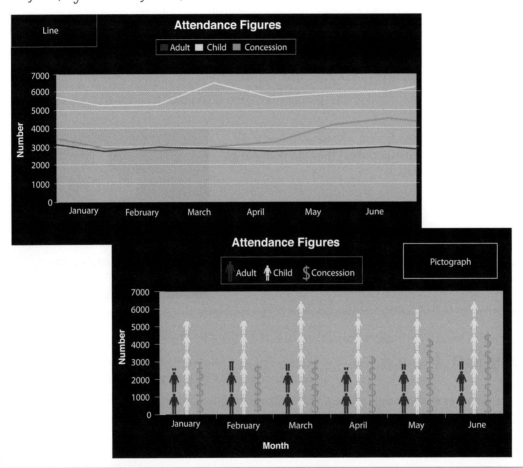

*You need to be able to suggest an alternative way of presenting data (rather than a spreadsheet or table). You also need to be able to say why they are better ways. You could choose from **line graphs, bar/column charts** or **pictographs**.*

Credit question 2 –

Marta Wisniewska works for Eastern European Food Imports. Part of her job is to prepare reports for the company managers.

Give two examples of the type of report that Marta might have to prepare, and suggest how she could ensure that the reports are professionally produced.

In this question, you need to be able to suggest what type of report might be produced in Eastern European Food Imports. There are many different types of report that Marta could prepare:

Marta could be asked to prepare a report on new security or Health and Safety procedures or on the company's financial performance for a given period.

To ensure that the reports are professionally produced, Marta should:
- *prepare them using word-processing software*
- *format them consistently throughout*
- *ensure that there are no spelling/grammar/layout mistakes in the final report*
- *incorporate tables, charts, graphs, pictures as appropriate to help explain what is being reported and make the report look more interesting.*

- *On the company's financial performance for a given period.*
- *On new security or Health and Safety procedures.*
- *On the type of imports from various suppliers.*
- *On the company's plans for growth.*
- *Stating why the company has decided to implement a new system.*

Any two examples that could be relevant to the company mentioned would be acceptable.

Look out for

The question asks for two examples of report. It does not state how many suggestions you should make on producing the reports professionally. Be guided by the number of marks in the question – each suggestion would get **1** mark.

Credit question 3 – ⊕

Jim has to give a presentation to the senior managers each month to keep them up to date on how sales are progressing against targets. He is a very busy man, and each month he just stands up and tells them how things are going.

He has now received complaints from the senior managers because they find it difficult to take in all that he is telling them, they have to try and take notes during the presentation and they sometimes forget some of what he has said.

Recommend two ways in which Jim could improve his presentation. Justify your answer.

Recommendation: Use a flipchart
Justification: To make a note of points raised during the presentation so that they can be discussed at the end.

Recommendation: Use an overhead projector
Justification: To let the audience see the information clearly.

Ways of improving a presentation. Use:

• Presentation software to enhance the quality of the presentation.
• Scanner/digital camera.
• TV/video.
• A flipchart.
• Word-processing/spreadsheet/DTP software to produce printouts and handouts (which could include graphics if relevant).
• Overhead projector/data projector.

Your justification for using these methods could be anything appropriate, for example:
• improved quality of presentation
• makes the presentation more interesting
• production of handouts and notes
• use of sound and effects to add interest
• use of video and pictures where appropriate
• ensures that people can see the information clearly
• allows the presenter to take notes of questions asked.

❗ Look out for

If you recommend a type of software, just recommend one type – you would not get 3 marks for listing three different types separately.

Similarly, if you suggest an overhead projector or a data projector, just suggest one or the other. You would not get 2 marks for mentioning both.

Credit question 4 –

You have recently started work as an administrator at Wilson Electronics plc. You have noticed that the company either does not have forms for routine tasks or is using very old versions of forms. You decide to suggest that the company forms are improved and brought up to date.

Identify two different forms that could be made available for general staff use. Justify the use of the forms identified.

- **Form**: Expenses Claim Form
  Justification: Anyone reading the form can quickly find the information they require about the expense being claimed.

- **Form**: Accident Report Form
  Justification: It will help ensure that staff give all the relevant information about the accident.

You should be aware of a range of different forms that are used by organisations, e.g.:

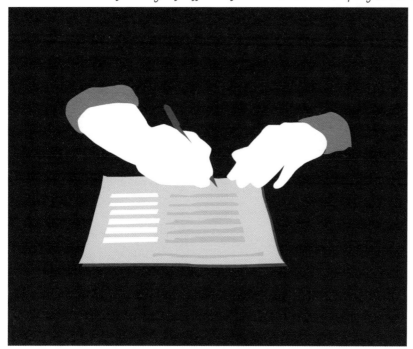

- Accident Report Forms
- Fax cover sheet
- Itineraries
- Travel and accommodation request forms
- Holiday request forms
- Expenses claim forms

Other justifications that could be given for using forms include:
- Once staff are used to the forms, these are quick to fill in.
- Staff get used to the form layout and know where the different bits of information go.
- The presentation of the form can be clearly laid out using word-processing software.

Arrangements

What you need to know at **General** **level …**

You need to know how to:

▶ arrange a business trip, e.g. dates, modes of transport, numbers, venues

▶ complete travel documents, e.g. itineraries, booking forms.

With the increase in the use of the internet and electronic communication, global markets are now available to everyone. Business travel, both home and overseas, is important to organisations as they deal with their customers and suppliers. Staff will attend meetings and conferences, visit trade fairs and exhibitions, or visit other branches of the organisation.

Making travel arrangements requires gathering lots of information and organising trips while making the most efficient uses of time, resources and finance. Sourcing the information means making use of the internet, travel guides, AA guides, maps, timetables and, when necessary, travel agents.

There are also important forms to complete to ensure that there are no mistakes. Choosing the correct method of travel depends on the purpose of the trip, who is travelling, when, the distance and the budget available. Many documents also need to be prepared and taken on business trips, e.g. passports, visas and itineraries.

General question 1 –

Your boss is making a visit to Pakistan. In addition to an itinerary, identify and describe three other essential pieces of documentation he must take with him.

Document 1 *Passport*

Description *This document is required as proof of identity and to allow travel outside the UK.*

Document 2 *Visa*

Description *Some countries outside Europe require this document for entry. Sometimes it will limit the time you are allowed to stay in the country.*

Document 3 *Immunisation form*

Description *If you are visiting a country in Africa or Asia, this proves that you have had injections against some diseases.*

When answering this question, you need to recognise that the trip is to a country outside Europe. Therefore it is important to mention documents such as visas and immunisation forms, as well as passports, travel insurance and flight tickets. It would not be correct to mention the EHIC (European Health Insurance Card) in this answer, as this is only for use within Europe. Your answer should name a document and then describe its purpose.

Look out for

You need to make sure that you know the full range of travel documents and also the type of information that they contain.

General question 2 –

As the Admin Assistant, you have the responsibility for arranging business trips for the organisation's employees. Recently, a few problems have arisen. Consider **each** of the following problems and make a suggestion to improve the situation.

- Joe Simpson in Accounts missed an important meeting held in central London, as his flight was delayed by two hours at Edinburgh airport. By the time he had reached London, collected his baggage and travelled into town, the whole trip had taken him nearly five hours.
- Lizzy Markham, the HR Manager, was booked on a car ferry from Portpatrick to Larne despite the fact that she is terrified of sailing.
- Alan Rose, the Sales Manager, was furious to find himself in a bed-and-breakfast guest house on a recent business trip to Leeds.
- Enid Reid, the Mail Room Supervisor, had a very difficult time at airport check-in recently, as she thought she had lost her ticket. All she had was a computer printout.

Suggestion 1

Joe might be better to travel by train to meetings in London, as the train goes from city centre to city centre. He could also go down the night before if necessary to ensure that he gets to his meeting on time.

Suggestion 2

Lizzy should have completed a Travel Request Form highlighting her fear of travel by sea. It might be better for her to fly and hire a car in future.

Suggestion 3

Alan should have completed a Travel and Accommodation Request Form. It is the responsibility of the Admin Assistant to check the allowances that each grade of employee can spend on overnight accommodation to make sure that they are booked into the right type of accommodation.

Suggestion 4

It is important to update staff regularly on any changes to travel procedures, for example the use of e-tickets, which are really just printouts of internet pages.

This question is about knowing the facts about who is travelling and being aware of any special requirements that need to be addressed – for example, what the most efficient and effective method of travel is and the advantages of travelling by rail as opposed to flying. It is also the duty of the Admin Assistant to check the travel allowances of each member of staff so that they are booked into the correct level of accommodation. It is also important to check if they have any special requirements, for example disabled access, vegetarian meals or requests for internet access. The Admin Assistant also needs to update staff on changes to travel procedures.

Look out for

Be prepared to complete a Travel Request Form, Travel and Accommodation Booking Form, Itinerary or an Expenses Claim Form from information given to you in a question.

General question 3 – ⊕

Rahat Aziz is a recruitment consultant and has a meeting in Birmingham on Tuesday 2 June. She is flying with British Midland from Edinburgh airport, check-in desk 9.

Flight Times:

Mon 01 Jun	Tue 02 Jun	Wed 03 Jun
WW 1001 dep. 07:00, arr. 08:20	WW 1001 dep. 0900, arr. 10:20	WW 1001 dep. 07:00, arr. 08:20
WW 1003 dep. 15:55, arr. 17:10	WW 1003 dep. 15:55, arr. 17:10	WW 1003 dep. 15:55, arr. 17:10
WW 1005 dep. 19:30, arr. 20:40	WW 1005 dep. 19:30, arr. 20:40	WW 1005 dep. 19:30, arr. 20:40

Additional Information

Her first appointment is to have lunch with David Patterson, HR Manager of Elliots Recruitment. This has been arranged for 12:15 pm at Gino's Trattoria, 26 Charlotte Street and is expected to last two hours.

Her second appointment is to visit the Elliots Recruitment Agency, which is just around the corner in Brooks Street. She has a meeting with Elaine Hay to discuss recent Equal Opportunities legislation. It is anticipated that this meeting will last for about 1.5 hours.

After this, Rahat wants to get back to Edinburgh as soon as possible.

Complete the itinerary for Rahat's trip using all of the information above.

❗ Look out for

When completing forms, always try to keep your answers as neat as possible.

*This requires you to read the information carefully and then put it into the correct place within the itinerary on the next page. You will be expected to know that you need to give the **name of the person** the itinerary is for and the **dates** of the trip. All times must be shown in the **24-hour clock.** You must also provide information on check-in times and flight numbers. Contact details of the people she will be meeting and addresses should be included. You will also be expected to allow time for travelling.*

ITINERARY FOR .Rahat Aziz.........................

VISIT TO .Birmingham.............................

ON .Tuesday 2nd June..............................

Time		Details
0530	Hours	Taxi to airport
	Hours	Check in .08 00 hours.................
	Hours	Depart .09.00 hours.................
	Hours	Arrive .10 20 hours...............
	Hours	Lunch .12 15 hours...............
		.David Patterson..................
		.Gino's Trattoria..................
	Hours	Meeting .14.30 hours..............
		.Elaine Hay......................
		.Elliots Recruitment Agency, Brooks Street.
	Hours	Check in .18.30 hours...............
	Hours	Depart .19.30 hours................
	Hours	Arrive .20 40 hours............

Check-in should **not** be **less than 30 mins** before the flight departs. The correct times should be extracted from the data given, and flight numbers should be added.

The **time** for lunch – **who** Rahat is meeting and **where** should be recorded.

The **time, place** and name of the person Rahat is meeting after lunch.

General question 4 – ⊛

You are the Admin Assistant to Gael Higgins, Human Resources Manager of Rosebank plc. She will be attending a conference at Head Office in Bristol from Wednesday 18 June to Friday 20 June. She e-mails you the following information.

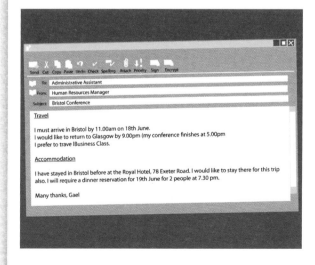

Send Cut Copy Paste Undo Check Spelling Attach Priority Sign Encrypt

To: Administrative Assistant
From: Human Resources Manager
Subject: Bristol Conference

Travel

I must arrive in Bristol by 11.00am on 18th June.
I would like to return to Glasgow by 9.00pm (my conference finishes at 5.00pm)
I prefer to travel Business Class.

Accommodation

I have stayed in Bristol before at the Royal Hotel, 78 Exeter Road. I would like to stay there for this trip also. I will require a dinner reservation for 19th June for 2 people at 7.30 pm.

Many thanks, Gael

Look out for

Details of the flight Rahat is able to get home.

You access the following flight information and complete the Travel and Accommodation Form.

FLIGHT TIMETABLE – Simply Flights					
Glasgow – Bristol					
Monday to Friday			**Saturdays and Sundays**		
Flight No.	Depart	Arrive	Flight No.	Depart	Arrive
SF1465	0845 hours	1000 hours	SF1463	0945 hours	1100 hours
SF1467	1515 hours	1630 hours	SF1469	1635 hours	1750 hours
SF1471	2050 hours	2205 hours			
FLIGHT TIMETABLE – Simply Flights					
Bristol – Glasgow					
Monday to Friday			**Saturdays and Sundays**		
Flight No.	Depart	Arrive	Flight No.	Depart	Arrive
SF1464	0705 hours	0820 hours	SF1468	1435 hours	1550 hours
SF1466	1335 hours	1450 hours	SF1474	2010 hours	2125 hours
SF1472	1910 hours	2025 hours			

Travel and Accommodation Order Form				
Employee Details				
Name	*Gael Higgins*			
Job Title	*Human Resources Manager*			
Travel				
Departing From	*Glasgow*	To	*Bristol*	Return/~~Single~~
Outward Journey				
Departure Date		Departure Time		
Return Journey				
Return Date		Return Time		
Preferred form of travel				
Special Requests				
Highlight the important information in the e-mail				
Accommodation				
Name and Address of Accommodation				
Number of Nights		Special Requests		
Signed		Date		

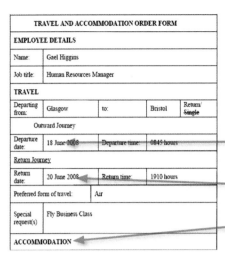

TRAVEL AND ACCOMMODATION ORDER FORM					
EMPLOYEE DETAILS					
Name:	Gael Higgins				
Job title:	Human Resources Manager				
TRAVEL					
Departing from:	Glasgow	to:		Bristol	Return/ ~~Single~~
	Outward Journey				
Departure date:	18 June 2008	Departure time:		0845 hours	
Return Journey					
Return date:	20 June 2008	Return time:		1910 hours	
Preferred form of travel:		Air			
Special request(s)		Fly Business Class			
ACCOMMODATION					

When you are expected to complete a form, it is important to make sure that you note how many boxes you are expected to fill in. The first part of the form has been completed for you, so the marks will be allocated to the Outward Journey dates and times, the Return Journey dates and times, the preferred mode of travel, the Special Request, and accommodation details.

You are provided with an e-mail and a flight schedule – you will be expected to use them both. You will never be given something that is unnecessary to the question. If you have a highlighter pen, or even just with your pen, mark the important information in the e-mail and schedule that you are going to need. This way, you should be able to complete the form with the correct details.

Note: You will not be expected to sign or date the form.

Be careful with this type of question because, although it looks easy, you will usually have to work quite hard to get all the marks. It would be unlikely that you would get a mark for every piece of information correctly completed. It may be that you would only get 1 mark for the departure details being correct, for example, and 1 mark for the special requests.

It is also a good idea to check over the form to make sure that you have completed all the boxes.

What you need to know at Credit **level ...**

In addition to what you need to know at General level, you should be able to give

▶ an evaluation of travel arrangements.

Credit question 1 –

Suggest three items you would include in a checklist for organising worldwide business trips. Justify why you would include these particular items.

The first part of this question is straightforward, but the second part, which asks you to justify, is where you will get most marks. You must make sure that you state why you have included the item in the checklist.

1 **Suggest:** Travel and Accommodation Request Form
Justification: This will ensure that all their requirements are noted and there is less likely to be any error in bookings if this is used, and that all incorrect expenses can be repaid at that no documents are forgotten.

Look out for

Be aware of other sources of information apart from the internet which can be used to help make travel arrangements, e.g. maps, timetables, CD-ROMs and travel agents.

2 Always check the **budget** available for the trip.
   Justification: This will ensure that the correct type of hotels and methods of transport are booked.

3 Ensure that the correct **documentation** is in place for the trip.
   Justification: If the trip is abroad, a **passport, EHIC, visa, currency, travel insurance** and **itinerary** may be needed.

Credit question 2 –

Eilidh McLean, the Admin Assistant at Patterson Enterprises has received the following e-mail from her boss, Peter Murphy.

> To: emclean@pattersonenterprises.co.uk
>
> Cc:
>
> Subject: Trip to Prague
>
> Eilidh
> I am going to attend a business meeting in Prague next week, Tuesday to Friday. I want to stay in a 4-star hotel near to the centre of the city. Can you make all the necessary arrangements?
>
> Thanks
> Peter

Eilidh has never organised trips before and is not sure where to start. Suggest three steps she could take, **justifying** why **each** of these steps is important in this process.

*This question requires that you **evaluate** what needs to be done in order to arrange business travel. Again, the difficult bit is to justify the advice that you will be giving. You will need to give a different justification in each case and will not gain full marks if you don't do this. There are more than three steps, so a number of different answers may be acceptable here.*

1 Get Peter to complete a Travel and Accommodation Request Form.
   Justification: This will mean that Eilidh will then be able to ensure that she has all the necessary information regarding the dates of travel, the preferred type of travel, accommodation and any other special requests.

2 Use the internet to search for a suitable 4-star hotel in Prague – use the video clips and traveller reviews to help make a decision.
   Justification: This will let Eilidh compare prices and, using the map facilities, check exactly where the hotel is located.

3 Check that Peter has an up-to-date passport, insurance and a European Health Insurance Card.
   Justification: This will ensure that he should have a trouble-free time getting through customs, and, if he does have any medical or other problems, then he has the correct documentation.

Paying for travel

South East Essex College
of Arts & Technology
Luker Road, Southend-on-Sea Essex SS1 1ND
Tel:(01702) 220400 Fax:(01702) 432320 Minicom: (01702) 220642

What you need to know at General **and** Credit **level ...**

You need to know how to

▶ pay for travel, e.g. cash, cheque, credit card, debit card

▶ use expense claim forms.

If your job in an organisation requires you to travel regularly, either within the UK or abroad, this will mean that from time to time you may have to pay for items out of your own pocket. Organisations will normally issue business credit and debit cards. These allow employees to buy goods and services while on company business, and the bill will be sent straight to the Finance Department to settle. Business cards allow the organisation to control spending, and limits can be placed on cards to ensure that the employee does not spend more than they are allowed to.

However, if the employee does use their own money, they can usually claim back any expenses incurred on their return as long as they complete a Travel Expense Claim Form and attach relevant receipts.

For the first part of this questions, you are being tested to see that you know the quickest and most efficient way to get to Rome for a two-day trip.

For the second part of the question, you are expected to be able to suggest the best method of payment in each of the given situations. The point to remember is that not all restaurants accept credit cards, and it is useful to have cash or the local currency to pay for small items of expenditure.

General question 1 –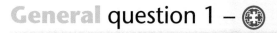

The Marketing Manager in your organisation is attending a two-day Trade Fair in Rome.

a) Suggest the best form of travel to use for this trip.
   Air

b) During the trip, she will have various expenses. In each of the following situations suggest the best possible method of payment:

   A taxi from the airport to the hotel in Rome
   A taxi would usually require payment in cash.

   Dinner at a small local restaurant
   Debit card/cash

   Coffee and a snack at the Trade Fair
   Cash

   The hotel bill for the two-day stay.
   Credit card

*Dinner at a small local restaurant suggests that it might not accept credit cards, so a **debit card/ cash** might be more appropriate here; also, if the dinner is more expensive than your allowance, you will not be able to claim the extra expense from the organisation.*

 **Look out for**

Remember that the euro is the currency used throughout most of the European Union.

Credit question 1 – ⊕

a) Describe two benefits to the employee and employer of using business credit cards.
b) Justify why a spreadsheet should be used rather than manual Travel Expense Claim Forms to record employee expenses.

---

a) *Benefits to the **employee**:*
- *They do not need to carry around large sums of cash.*
- *They will not be out of pocket for business expenses.*

*Benefits to the **employer**:*
- *A spending limit can be placed on the credit card which will stop employees from spending too much money.*
- *Statements of Account sent at the end of each month are usually itemised and will clearly show what the employee has spent.*

b) *In the Travel Expense Claim Form, you are expected to calculate items like daily expenditure on food, petrol or travel – using formulae in spreadsheets would make this automatic, which would reduce the chance of human error. The spreadsheet could be accessed on the organisation's intranet and then sent by e-mail to the Finance staff, who should find it easier to check, thus making it more accessible and quicker to process. It also reduces the amount of paper.*

Credit question 2 – ⊕

Suggest and justify two reasons for checking and verifying business expenses.

Two reasons to check and verify business expences are:
i) to make sure that receipts submitted and claims match so that no-one is under or over-paid.
ii) to check for accuracy and to make sure that all claims are within budgets and allowances set by the organisation.

For part a) of this question, you must clearly differentiate the benefits that the employee will gain from those that the employer will gain.

*Part b) of this question is connected to your understanding of ICT, and in particular spreadsheets. But you also need to know what is usually contained in a Travel Expense Claim Form. As this is a **justify** question, you will need to state clearly the benefits of using a spreadsheet.*

To ensure that the business traveller is not out of pocket for any monies paid out during their trip, it is important to make the process of claiming back expenses as efficient and effective as possible. In this question, you would need to make sure that, for each reason given, you explain why this process exists. For example:
- *All Travel Expense Claim Forms should be checked for accuracy of data input and the calculation of totals. The reason for this is that any data-entry error or over-calculation could result in the employee receiving more or less money back than they are entitled to.*
- *Forms should be checked to ensure that totals claimed are within budget allocations and receipts have been provided. The reason for this is that, if control is not kept on expenditure, then there could be problems later with departmental finance. Receipts provide proof of what is being claimed for.*